ALL ABOUT CRIBBAGE

All About
Cribbage

by <u>Douglas Anderson</u>

BAILEY BROTHERS AND SWINFEN LTD.
Folkestone

Published in Great Britain by
BAILEY BROTHERS AND SWINFEN LIMITED

The author gratefully acknowledges the assistance so freely given by friends, libraries, and other agencies. Particular thanks go to Murille Schofield of Gaspereaux for the research he did for me ... to Arnold Sarty and Gordon Bauld, both of Halifax, for their useful comments and suggestions ... and to George Baker of Kentville, for making the mathematical calculations and providing the tables in the last chapter.

1974

SBN 561 00211 8

1st Reprint 1975

Printed in Great Britain by
Whitstable Litho Ltd., Whitstable, Kent

To my good friend Herbert M. Stairs,
a gentleman and sportsman of merit,
with whom I have enjoyed
many games of Cribbage.

Foreword

By Henry D. Hicks, C. C., Q. C.

It amazes me to discover that, though the game of cribbage dates back some 350 years, there is not in print today a single comprehensive book dealing with the game. G. Douglas Anderson's book fills the gap admirably, starting with the history of cribbage from Sir John Suckling's time, and including chapters dealing most comprehensively with all aspects of the play of the modern game.

According to his friend, John Aubrey, Suckling was "the greatest gallant of his time." Aubrey tells us further that because of his reputation as a "gamester both for bowling and cards . . . no shopkeeper would trust him for sixpence, as today for instance he might by winning be worth £200 and the next day he might not be worth half so much, or perhaps be sometimes minus nihilo."

Whether today's reader is going to play cribbage so avidly as to jeopardize his credit rating with his banker, or only play a friendly game with his wife, he will find this book highly interesting and altogether helpful.

Of especial interest to the more serious player will be the chapters dealing with the odds and chances, which have never before been calculated and presented in such a compact and easily understandable form.

Assuredly there must be more to learn about the game of cribbage and the play of the cards, but this book will carry the beginner or the seasoned player a long way toward becoming a "cribbage expert."

Table of Contents

ALL ABOUT CRIBBAGE

Chapter I

A Brief History

The origin of playing cards is obscure. Some historians attribute their beginning to China, Egypt, or India, while others make out a strong case for their use in fourteenth-century Europe. There is some evidence that the Crusaders, who were inveterate gamblers, learned about cards from the Arabs, but maybe it was vice versa. In 1423 St. Bernadino of Siena, in a famous sermon preached at Bologna, traced their origin back to the Devil. The Puritans who came later agreed with him.

We do know that they were popular 572 years ago, for the Edict of the Provost of Paris in 1397 forbade working people to play tennis, bowls, dice, cards, or ninepins on working days. (Since medieval man usually had one day off in three, due to numerous feasts, celebrations, and holy days, there was possibly good reason for this restriction.)

Most of the earliest playing cards were rectangular or square, but sometimes they were round. At the beginning of the fifteenth century there were 78 cards to a pack in Venetian Italy, 22 emblematic and 56 numerical. By the middle of the fifteenth century the French had reduced the number to the now standard 52 and the present four suits. Early German cards showed hearts, bells, leaves, and acorns. Later cards depicted swords, batons, cups, money, animals, flowers, and human figures.

Playing cards were put to many uses besides gaming. In 1509 a Franciscan friar, Thomas Murner, published an exposition in logic in the form of a pack of cards. In 1651 Baptiste Pendelton used a deck to teach grammar. Men concerned with geography, history, and even current politics used cards as a medium to teach and influence the public. The so-called Popish Plot in England was one of the subjects so illustrated.

Cards became big business. In Russia their manufacture was a government monopoly. In England in 1463, Edward IV forbade their importation from abroad as it was "hurting trade," and in 1615 James

I tacked on the first duty, six shillings to a gross of packs.

In the New World cards are first heard of in the letters of Herra, a companion of Cortez. He describes the interest of the Aztecs in the games of the Spanish soldiers. Today, in North America, playing cards are to be found in more than 90 percent of all homes, and in many other places as well.

The Immortal Hoyle

Edmond Hoyle, an Englishman, was born in 1679 and, even though he was buried in 1769 at the ripe old age of ninety, today his influence is wider than it ever was. In 1746 Hoyle published a book which contained the rules of five different games and short treatises on them. The book was called *Hoyle's Games*. It was the only book he ever published, and it was a popular one—so popular that within a few years other writers were putting Hoyle's name on books which they themselves had written about games. Over the years, hundreds of such books have appeared. Even though Hoyle was buried two hundred years ago, new books by him continue to appear—written from the grave, as it were. (Bohn's *Handbook of Games,* published in 1850, contains a complete reprint of Hoyle's book on games.)

3

To many people, Hoyle is still a very real and living person. They may not know where, but they are sure that he lives and can be reached by mail or phone.

Who Invented Cribbage?

We can thank Sir John Suckling, an Englishman whose life span covered the years 1609 to 1642, for the invention of cribbage. In *The Compleat Gamester* by Cotton, published in 1674, the game was called "Cribbidge." Since that time only the spelling of the name and some of the terminology have changed. The original rules and method of scoring are exactly the same as they were in Suckling's day. This is quite a tribute to his expertness and skill. He was a very meticulous person and, since cribbage was intended as a gambling game, he provided a set of rules that was very complete and detailed. (See Chapter VIII, "The Rules of Cribbage.")

Actually, cribbage evolved out of an earlier game called "Noddy." In early cribbage a Jack in the crib was called "Knave Noddy." Later it was called "His Nobs." Today many call it "His Nibs" or "His Heels," although an increasing number of players simply call it "the Jack."

Suckling cut quite a swath in his day. He attended Trinity College in Cambridge, spent several years in France and Italy, and returned to England in 1630 to be knighted by the King. Suckling was wealthy, having inherited his father's fortune when he was only eighteen. He was basically a poet and playwright, but he was also a soldier, and fought under Gustavus Adolphus in the Battle of Brietenfeld and in many sieges. In 1639, at his own expense, he raised a troop of one hundred horse and accompanied King Charles I and his poorly trained force on the ill-fated Scottish expedition, or Bishop's War.

He is described as being rich, handsome, generous, and popular. He was elected to Parliament, was a favourite in the King's court and in the great castles and country homes of England, and was regarded as the best card player and bowler in Britain, if not in all Europe. He had many friends, and two of the closest were John Hales and Sir William Davenant. These two were also great friends of John Aubrey, a sometime historian, sometime gossip monger, whom they furnished with a great deal of information about Suckling and other people. They told Aubrey about the new card game called "cribbage" which Suckling had originated, and how popular it was becoming with the gentlemen who sat at the gaming tables.

Sir John came to an early end. In 1641 he led a

conspiracy to rescue a friend who was incarcerated in the Tower of London. The plot was discovered and Sir John fled to France where, a year later, fearing poverty and unable to return to England, he took poison and died.

Chapter II

The Game of Cribbage

Cribbage is unquestionably the best card game for two players that was ever developed. It has the further advantage of being an equally enthralling game for three or four players.

Cribbage differs from most other card games because of the tremendous number and variety of chances to score both in the play and in the count of the hand and crib.

The game consists of either 61 or 121 points. The points are scored on a cribbage board. In five-card cribbage, 61 points always constitute the game. During the early years of the game, either

61 or 121 counted as game for six-card cribbage. Modern usage has settled on 121, and most cribbage boards are now made to conform to that count.

The complete pack of fifty-two cards is used. The cards rank downwards from the face cards, which all count 10, to Ace, which counts 1. The cards in between are all counted at their face value.

The five-card game with two players was the original game, the root stock from which the other forms of the game have sprung. Years ago it was said that five-card cribbage provided the greatest challenge to the players and required the greatest skill. But the five-card game has been obsolete for many years; it did not stand the test of time. Cribbage players everywhere found the six-card game more satisfactory, and it has become the standard the world over.

No book on cribbage would be complete without a description of the five-card game. After all, it was the parent stem and all the other forms of the game are based upon it. It was a fast-moving game which perhaps suited the tempo of the time it was created and appealed to the people who played it in those days. (A description of this game is included in Chapter V, "Other Cribbage Games," beginning on p. 41.) It is suggested that you give this game a trial. It will prove a very interesting change of pace from the usual six-card game.

This book describes in detail the six-card game. It also shows how this game may be played by three players, each independent of the others, and by four players playing as two pairs of partners.

The Cribbage Board

The cribbage board that is in general use today provides a complete row of 120 holes for each player and one "game hole," a starting box for the pegs before play has started, and a clearly marked "skunk" line. In addition, the row of holes across one end of the board provides a place for each player to keep a record of the number of games won.

The board is placed between the players. To mark the progress of the game each player has two pegs. (The pairs are usually of different colours.)

At the start of the game the pegs should be put in the holes in the four-hole starting box. The two holes on the outside are for one player and the two on the inside for the other. Similarly, the row of holes around the outside of the board is to be used by one player, the inside row by the other.

If the first player to score makes 2 points, that player will move one of his pegs into the second hole of the first block of five. If that player's next score is 3, he will move his *other* peg from the

9

starting box and place it in the third hole ahead of the peg with which he previously scored 2. Whenever that player scores he removes the back peg and, counting from the front peg, places it in the appropriate hole. And so the marking of the scoring continues until the game hole has been reached by one player.

The number of holes between the player's two pegs indicates the amount he has last scored. The position of the front peg always indicates his total progress in the game as well as his position relative to that of his opponent. The front peg must not be disturbed, because the distance between the pegs allows the players to check each other's scores.

A player should never touch his opponent's pegs.

The Play of the Game

In two-handed cribbage the cards are shuffled and the cut for deal is made. The dealer deals six cards alternately, one at a time, face down to each player. The players examine their hands, and decide which four cards to retain and which two to "lay away" face down in the crib. (See "Discarding for the Crib," p. 31.) The crib belongs to the dealer.

When the crib has been made, the non-dealer cuts the cards. The dealer then turns face up the top card of the lower deck, and this card is placed on top of the deck. This top card is called the "starter," or "turn-up card." (If the starter is a Jack, the dealer is entitled to peg 2 for "His Nob," but he must peg the 2 points before he has played his first card. See Chapter VIII, "The Rules of Cribbage," p. 65.)

The non-dealer begins the play by laying out one of his cards face up on the table in front of himself and calling out its value. (Aces are counted as 1's and all face cards as 10's.)

The dealer then lays a card from his hand in front of himself on the table, and calls out the sum of his opponent's card plus the card he has just played.

The non-dealer then plays another card, calling out the sum of the three cards that have been played. The dealer plays again in the same manner, and the play alternates thus until the sum of the cards played is 31, or until neither player can play a card without exceeding 31.

If a player plays a card that brings the total to exactly 31, he says "31," and pegs 2 points. If one player is unable to play another card without exceeding 31, he says "Go," and the other player must go on playing, if he can, until he reaches 31, or until he cannot play without exceeding 31. The player coming nearest to 31 scores a "Go," and is entitled to peg 1 hole.

After a Go or a 31 has been reached, each player turns the cards he has already played face down on the table in front of himself.

The play begins again with the remaining cards, with the first card played by the player who did not score. The counting again starts at zero and the play again alternates between the two players until another Go or 31 has been reached. Then the play will start again at zero, until all of the cards have been played.

The last card played scores 1 point, but if the last card makes a total of 31, 2 points only are pegged for the 31. (*It is only in this one case that the single point for the last card is not allowed.*)

When the cards dealt have all been played, the hands are counted. (See Chapter III, "Scoring," p. 13.) The non-dealer counts his score first. The dealer follows by counting his hand and then his crib. It is important that this order of counting be followed because near the end of the game the non-dealer may have sufficient points in his hand to "count out" and win the game before the dealer has a chance to count.

Thus the play continues, with the deal alternating between the two players, until one of them has gained the 121 points required for game.

Chapter III

Scoring

Scoring is accomplished in three ways:

Points earned during the play of the game.

Points representing the count of the hands and crib.

Points gained as a result of penalties and "Muggins."

Scoring During Play

The main object of the play is to score points by pegging. In addition to scoring 1 point for a Go or 2 points for a 31, points in play can also be made in the following ways: by making 15's, sequences or runs, pairs, pairs royal, double pairs royal, and by a Jack being the turn-up card or starter.

15's Every time you can play a card that makes the total of the play 15 you can peg 2 points. If your opponent starts the play with an 8, for example, you play a 7 and say, "15 for 2," and peg 2 points. The same would be true if you followed a 9 with a 6, a 5 with any one of the tenth cards, and so forth. (Fifteens can also be the sum of three or more cards, such as a 7 followed by a 6 and then by a 2.)

Pairs Playing a card of the same rank as the one last played is worth 2 points. (However, tenth cards pair only by similarity, that is, a Jack with a Jack or a 10 with a 10. A Queen does not make a pair with a King, even though they both have a counting rank of 10.)

Suppose your opponent starts the play with a 9. You play a 9, saying "18, and 2 for the pair," and peg 2 points. Then suppose your opponent plays an 8, saying "26," and you follow with a 2 for 28. If your opponent can't play another card without exceeding 31, he says "Go"—but your hand contains another 2, so you play it and say "30, and 2 for the pair and 1 for Go," and peg 3 points.

14

Pairs Royal or Three of a Kind or Triplets If, after a pair has been made, a third card of the same rank can be played immediately (provided, of course, that no Go or 31 has intervened), the player of the third card scores 6 points. (Tenth cards form triplets only if they are similar, such as three Jacks or three Kings.)

The 6 points are made up of 2 points for each of the three pairs that can be formed with three similar cards. (See Chapter VII, "Terms Used in Cribbage," p. 58.)

Double Pairs Royal or Four of a Kind or Double Pairs If, after a pairs royal has been made, another card of the same rank can be played immediately (provided that no Go or 31 has intervened), the player of the fourth card scores 12 points. (Obviously, double pairs royal can be scored only with cards whose rank is 7 or less.)

The 12 points are made up of 2 points for each of the six pairs that can be formed with the four similar cards. (See Chapter VII, "Terms Used in Cribbage," p. 58.)

Sequences or Runs When three or more cards in numerical sequence, but not necessarily of the same suit, are played the result is a sequence. The cards need not be played in order of sequence. If you lead the 6 of spades and your opponent follows with the 8 of diamonds, you can then play the 7 card of any suit for a count of 21, and score 3 points for the sequence. Your opponent can then play either a 5 or a 9 for a sequence of four cards and score 4 points—and the play can continue as long as a continuous sequence can be made without exceeding 31.

However, it is necessary to keep track of the order in which the cards are played to make sure that what looks like a sequence is not interrupted by a foreign card. The following two examples illustrate this point.

Suppose the cards are played in this order: 8, 7, 7, 6. The opponent started the play with an 8; the dealer followed with a 7 and said "15 for 2 points"; the opponent followed with a 7 and said "22, and 2 for the pair." The dealer then played a 6, but he cannot score for the sequence because it was broken by the second 7.

Now suppose the cards were played in this order, starting with the opponent: 9, 6, 8, 7. The dealer would score 2 points for the 15 after he played the 6, and 4 points for the sequence after he played the 7. While the four cards were not played in sequential order, they do form a four run or sequence with no foreign card intervening. In this example, the opponent has not gained any score.

If a break in a sequence is filled without the

intervention of a "foreign" card the player who completes the sequence pegs 1 for each card in the completed sequence. For example: The dealer holds K, 3, 2, A. The opponent holds Q, 6, 5, 4. The following illustration shows the order in which all the cards were played and the scoring:

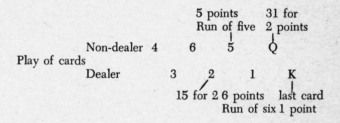

Sequences can also be made with cards played by only one player. Here is an example which demonstrates this point, and also demonstrates the value of holding a run of low cards in your hand for as long as possible. Suppose you are dealer and hold a 10, 3, 2 and A. Your opponent, holding 6, 7, 8, and 9, starts the play with 7; you follow with your 10 for 17; he plays his 6 for 23. You play your 3 for 26, and your opponent says "Go." You then play your 2 and A for a run of three and count 3 for the run and 1 for the Go.

Ace is always low, counting as 1, and can form a sequence only with a 2. It cannot form a sequence with a King.

17

Similarly, "tenth" cards cannot be treated as a group in forming sequences. That is, 8, 9, Q do not form a sequence; but 8, 9, 10, J or 10, J, Q, K do.

Flush A flush cannot happen in the play of the cards. It occurs only when computing the hands and crib.

Scoring of Hands and Crib

The starter or turn-up card is common property of both players and is used by both players in computing the value of their hands and the crib. After all the cards have been played, the non-dealer places his four cards face up on the table and counts his hand together with the starter. He makes as many scoring combinations as possible, announces his count aloud, and then pegs the correct number of holes for the total value of his hand and the turn-up card.

Then the dealer counts his score, first with his hand and the starter, then with the crib and the starter.

Points in the hands or crib can be made by 15's, pairs, pairs royal, double pairs royal, sequences or runs, flushes, and by having the Jack in the hand or crib that is of the same suit as the turn-up card.

15's Every combination of cards that totals 15 counts 2 points. For example, if your hand contains a King, Queen, and a 5, it has two 15's. If in addition the turn-up card is a tenth card, your hand has three 15's. If the turn-up card is a 5, then you have four 15's for a count of 8, plus a pair for 10.

Pairs Each pair of cards in the hand counts 2 points. Of course, the turn-up card is considered a part of the hand, and is used to assist you in pairing.

Pairs Royal or Three of a Kind or Triplets Three cards of the same rank held in the hand, or with the assistance of the turn-up card, counts for 6 points. (See Chapter VII, "Terms Used in Cribbage," p. 58.)

Double Pairs Royal or Four of a Kind or Quadruplets Four cards of the same rank held in the hand, or with the assistance of the turn-up card, counts for 12 points. (See Chapter VII, "Terms Used in Cribbage," p. 58.)

Sequences or Runs Each combination of three or more cards in sequence of rank, regardless of suit, with or without the assistance of the turn-up card, counts 1 point for each card. If your hand contains a 6, 7, and 8 and the turn-up card is a 7, you have two separate runs of three, for which you count 6 points, plus 2 for the pair of 7's. You also have two 15's, for which you count 4 points. Or if your hand contains a 4, 5, 6, and 7 and the turn-up card is a 4, you have two runs of 4 for 8 points, plus 2 for the pair of 4's. In addition, the sum of the two sequences of 4, 5, 6 make 2 15's, and the two 4's and the 7 make another 15, for a total of 16 points.

Thus, it can be seen that a double run of three counts 8 points and a double run of four counts 10 points.

A triple run of three, such as 2, 3, 4, 4, 4 counts 15; 9 points for the three runs of three and 6 points for the pairs royal.

A quadruple run of three (two different cards duplicated) such as 2, 3, 3, 4, 4, counts 16; 12 points for the four runs of three and 4 points for the two pairs. Of course if 15's are also involved they add further to the count.

Remember, though, that tenth cards cannot be treated as a group. If your hand contains a 7, 8, 9, and 10 and the turn-up card is a Queen, your hand contains one sequence of four for 4 points. The 7 and 8 also make a 15 for 2 points. Even though the turn-up card is a tenth card, it cannot count as a 10 for a double run of four. To form a proper sequence of five, the turn-up card would have to be a Jack or a 6.

Flush Four cards of the same suit in the hand count for 4 points. Should the turn-up card also be of the same suit, the five-card flush counts for 5 points.

However, a flush in the crib does not count unless the turn-up card is the same suit as the four cards in the crib. It is important to remember the difference between a flush in the hand and a flush in the crib.

His Nob or Jack in the Hand or Crib Should either the hand or the crib contain the Jack of the same suit as the turn-up card, it counts for 1 point.

Points Made Through Penalties

If, during the course of the deal, the dealer exposes one of his own cards, no penalty is invoked; but if he exposes one of his opponent's cards, the opponent scores 2 points and may, in addition, demand a new deal provided he does so before turning over and looking at the rest of his cards.

Should a misdeal occur without the dealer being aware of it until one or both of the hands has been taken up, the opponent shall score 2 points and the cards must be shuffled and dealt again.

Should the dealer give his opponent more than the proper number of cards, there must be a new deal and the opponent scores 2 points, provided the error is discovered before the opponent picks up his cards. If the error is not discovered until after the opponent has picked up his cards, he cannot score the 2 points but there must be a new deal.

At the commencement of the game the players must decide whether the "lurch" or "skunk" shall apply. If it does, the game counts double if one player scores 121 points before his opponent has scored 91. If double "lurch" or "skunk" is to apply, the game counts as four games if one player scores 121 before his opponent scores 61.

When the deal has been completed, the pack that was dealt from shall not be touched by any player until the time has come to cut for the "start" of play. Should a player touch the deck, the opposing player scores 2 points.

Should either player confuse his cards with the crib, the other player scores 2 points and calls for a new deal.

When the cut for the "start" has been made, should the turn-up card be a Jack, the dealer scores 2 points for "His Nob."

NOTE: Some players have the mistaken idea that the dealer may not score the 2 points if he is within 6 points of the game. This is not so. He scores the 2 points even if by so doing he reaches 121 points or game.

Should a player take, or peg, more points than he is entitled to when scoring for a penalty or when counting his hand or crib, he shall be set back the number of points he has overscored so that the scoring is corrected. In addition, his adversary adds the same number of points to his own score.

Should a player neglect to score points to which he is entitled as the result of a penalty or when counting his hand or crib, there is no penalty unless it has been agreed that "Muggins" will apply. In that case, the opposing player may say "Muggins" and then himself score the points overlooked.

Should a player touch the pegs of his adversary except to correct an error in score or should he touch his own pegs except when he has a right to score, he shall forfeit 2 points to his opponent.

Should both pegs of a player be displaced by accident, the opponent must be allowed to restore them to their places. Should the player refuse this right to his opponent, then the opponent may claim the game.

Should a player neglect to play when he could have "come in" under 31, his opponent may score 2 points.

Should a player, in error, score a game as won that he has not won, he forfeits the game.

Should a player refuse to pay any penalty he may have incurred by infringing the rules of play, his opponent may claim the game.

Counting

Experienced players have found that counting is facilitated and simplified if the summing up is done in the following order: 15's, sequences or runs, flushes, pairs or pairs royal or double pairs royal, and "His Nob."

With the almost countless combinations of cards that are possible in cribbage, the value of a hand or crib can range from 0 to 29. Twenty-nine is the perfect hand, the maximum possible. To get it you must hold in your hand or crib three 5's and a Jack, and the turn-up card must be the 5 of the same suit as your Jack.

Oddly enough, no hand or crib can make up a count of 19, 25, 26, or 27.

The average hand is 8 and the average crib is 4. No matter how good or bad you think your run of hands or cribs may be, it is a safe bet that if you keep a record of one hundred of them you will find the same average values.

The following list of cribbage hands and scores includes many that the beginner may find difficulty in counting. It may also be a good reference for seasoned players.

CRIBBAGE SCORES

1 – 1 – 2 – 2 – 3 = 16	5 – 5 –N – J – J = 21
1 – 2 – 3 – 3 – 3 = 15	2 – 6 – 7 – 7 – 8 = 16
1 – 4 – 4 – 4 –10 = 12	6 – 7 – 8 – 9 – 9 = 16
2 – 3 – 4 – 4 – 4 = 17	3 – 3 – 6 – 6 – 6 = 20
2 – 2 – 3 – 3 – 3 = 8	3 – 3 – 3 – 4 – 5 = 21
2 – 2 – 2 – 2 – 9 = 20	1 – 1 – 7 – 7 – 8 = 12
2 – 3 – 3 – 3 – 4 = 17	3 – 3 – 3 – 6 – 6 = 18
3 – 3 – 4 – 4 – 5 = 20	3 – 3 – 6 – 6 – 9 = 14
3 – 4 – 4 – 4 – 5 = 17	5 – 5 – 5 –N – J = 23
3 – 4 – 4 – 5 – 5 = 16	5 – 5 – 5 –10 –10 = 22
3 – 6 – 6 – 6 – 6 = 24	1 – 4 – 4 –N – 4 = 13
4 – 4 – 5 – 6 – 6 = 24	5 – 5 –10 –N –Q = 18
4 – 5 – 5 – 6 – 6 = 24	3 – 3 – 3 – 3 – 9 = 24
4 – 5 – 6 – 6 – 6 = 21	4 – 4 – 4 – 4 – 3 = 20
5 –N – 5 – 5 – 5s = 29	4 – 4 – 4 – 4 – 7 = 24
5 – 5 – 5 – 5 –10 = 28	1 – 7 – 7 – 7 – 7 = 24
5 – 5 –10 – J –Q = 17	4 – 4 – 4 – 7 – 7 = 20
6 – 6 – 9 – 9 – 9 = 20	4 – 4 – 7 – 7 – 7 = 14
6 – 9 – 9 – 9 – 9 = 20	3 – 3 – 4 – 5 – 5 = 20
6 – 6 – 7 – 7 – 8 = 20	1 – 1 – 6 – 7 – 7 = 12
7 – 7 – 7 – 8 – 9 = 21	2 – 6 – 6 – 7 – 7 = 12
7 – 8 – 8 – 8 – 8 = 20	3 – 4 – 4 – 4 – 4 = 20
7 – 7 – 7 – 8 – 8 = 20	7 – 7 – 7 – 1 – 1 = 20
7 – 7 – 8 – 8 – 9 = 24	5 – 5 – 5 – 4 – 6 = 23
7 – 8 – 8 – 9 – 9 = 20	1 – 1 – 6 – 7 – 8 = 13

N = "His Nobs"   s = turn-up card

Figures of Interest

The total number of different hands (four cards plus the starter) in cribbage is 2,598,960.

In this total there are 624 chances of getting a hand with four of a kind or double pairs royal. The number of chances of getting three of a kind or pairs royal is much greater, 54,912.

The chances of holding three of a kind and another pair (a tight or full house in poker) number 3,744. Two pairs are more probable. There are 123,552 chances of getting these. One pair is even more probable—there are 1,098,240 chances of holding a pair in the hand.

In the total number of possible hands there are 225,280 combinations which contain no count. They are called "bust hands" and almost one-tenth of all the possible hands fall in this category.

Chapter IV

Strategy

Cribbage is an offensive as well as a defensive game. To play it scientifically and well you have to shift your tactics from time to time during the play. If you have a substantial lead, you can afford to play carefully and defensively to maintain it. If you are behind, on the other hand, you will be forced to take risks to improve your position and balk your opponent in his efforts to score.

Leading and Playing Cards

At the commencement of play your objective should be to gain a Go or a 31. The 1 or 2 points

27

you so gain are very much to your advantage, because they save you double that number of points by keeping them from your opponent.

The safest card to lead is a 4 because the next player cannot make a 15. Any cards of lower rank are better held in the hand for later play because of the chances they offer to make a 15, a Go, or a 31. A tenth card is also a fairly safe lead, especially if it permits you to hold low cards for pegging.

Risky cards to lead are 7's and 8's, but there are times when it pays to lead one of them, especially if you have in your hand cards of similar or close rank to back them up. From an 8, 7, 7, lead a 7. Should the dealer play an 8 for 15 and 2 points, you can follow with your 8 for 23 and 2 points for the pair. Should the dealer play 7 for 14 and 2 points for the pair, you can follow with your other 7 for 21 and 6 points for the pairs royal.

A 5 is perhaps the worst card to lead because the large number (sixteen) of tenth cards gives your opponent too great an opportunity to make 15. If you hold a tenth card and a 5, lead the tenth card. If your opponent plays a 5 for 15 and 2 points, you can then play your 5 for 20 and 2 points for the pair.

If you hold a pair in your hand, it is usually good tactics to lead one of them. Should your opponent pair it for 2 points, it gives you a chance

28

to play the other card for pairs royal for 6 points. The odds are very great against your opponent also having a pair and playing the fourth card for double pairs royal, for 12 points. Your opponent is also limited by the fact that the rank of the cards cannot be greater than 7's or the fourth card would exceed 31, and thus could not be played.

Should your opponent lead a card which you can either pair or supplement with a card that will make 15, it is preferable to make the 15 for 2 points. Your opponent may have a pair and if you pair his lead, it will give him the opportunity to make pairs royal or three of a kind for 6 points. Even if the cards in your hand do not permit you to make a 15, it is often advisable to forego the 2 points for the pair by playing some other card widely separated in rank from the one led by your opponent, so that he cannot form a sequence or run. In cribbage terminology you "play off" (By so doing you are really not giving up 2 points—on the average based on mathematical odds, you are giving up only 1.66 points. See Chapter VI, "Statistics and Odds," p. 48.) On the other hand, should your cards be close in rank, *"play on"* by playing a card close in rank to his with the hope that his next card will form a sequence of three for 3 points and permit you to play a fourth card in the sequence for 4. Whether you play *off* or *on*

29

depends on your hand, your relative position in the game, and whether or not either you or your opponent is close to game.

During the play do not, if you can possibly help it, play a card to make the count 21. Remember there are sixteen tenth cards your opponent can play for 31.

Should you be forced to lead from a sequence of three or four cards, play the highest or lowest rather than a card from the middle of the sequence. This will tend to balk your opponent and at the same time provide you with a greater chance to score in the play that follows.

During the play of the game if you lay down a 6 to make the count 25, you give your opponent the opportunity to pair it for 31 and 4 points. The same is true should you play a 4 for 27, a 3 for 28, or a 2 for 29. Avoid these plays if you possibly can.

Records gathered during the play of thousands of games indicate that the average hand should contain 8 points and the average crib 4. The average amount which either player may peg during play is 5 for the dealer and 4 for the non-dealer. But these amounts cannot always be depended on because of the infinite variety of cards that may be held in the hands, as well as the order in which they are played. There are times when one player may peg little or nothing while his opponent may peg several times the normal amount.

Discarding for the Crib

One of the most important parts of the game is how to discard for the crib in the best way to aid your own cause and balk your opponent. While certain general rules apply, they cannot and should not always be followed. The possibilities of the hand, the stage of the game, and your relative position on the board are factors to be considered. A good deal of skill, science, and knowledge of the game are involved. There is no substitute for careful observation and experience in developing the skill or art of discarding.

For the dealer   It is important for the dealer to put the best possible cards in his crib, but at the same time he must retain in his hand the cards that offer the greatest opportunity for score. The choice is not always simple or clear-cut. Consideration must be given to each hand. When in doubt as to your choice of trying to improve hand or crib, it is well to favour the crib at the expense of the hand. The odds of the game show that the probable chances of gaining points in the crib are somewhat better than of gaining them in the hand. "Salting" the crib with the best possible cards is very much to the dealer's advantage.

A double run in the hand should be held. A

31

sequence or run of three or four should seldom be broken unless by so doing a higher count can be retained in the hand. Even this higher count must be weighed against the possibility of the turn-up card being of the same rank as one of the three (or four) cards, which would increase the value of the hand by at least 5 points. The stage of the game and your position have a bearing. If you are well ahead, you can afford to be conservative and hold the cards which give you the highest count. If you are behind, then you should probably gamble and hold the cards that form the sequence, with the hope that the turn-up card will materially improve the count in the hand.

If the hand is a poor one, it is best to keep those cards which offer the greatest chance for pegging. These are the cards of middle rank. The 5 is perhaps the best pegging card because of the possibilities of making a 15 with it for 2 points. One writer suggests that the 7, 8, 6, and 9 follow in about that order, but actually there is little difference. All of these are also excellent cards to put in your crib. Whether they should be kept in the hand or put in the crib depends on the rank of the other cards in the hand and, to some extent, on the position of the game.

If the hand contains an excess of high cards but has a low count, it is often good tactics to retain an

Ace or Deuce if possible. These low-rank cards often make possible a 31 for 2 points.

A list of the best cards to lay out in your own crib would include two 5's, a 5 and a 6, a 5 and a tenth card, a 2 and a 3, a 4 and an Ace, a 6 and a 9, a 7 and an 8, or any pair. If you don't have any pairs or cards that make 15's, lay out "touching cards" such as an 8 and a 9, a 3 and a 4, or a 10 and a Jack. If even this is not possible, lay out cards that are as close in rank as possible, because this gives your crib a better chance of being assisted by the cards put in it by your opponent and also by the turn-up card. Of course, it is always best to put two cards of the same suit in your crib rather than two cards of the same rank but different suits. This gives you the additional chance, however slight, of getting a flush in the crib.

For the opponent or non-dealer   The non-dealer must endeavour to lay out cards which will do the most to balk the dealer—that is, cards that will be the least likely to be of advantage in producing scoring possibilities such as sequences or 15's in the crib.

A 5 is probably the least desirable card to put in the dealer's crib because it makes a 15 for 2 points with any one of the sixteen cards that have a value of 10. Unless it is to the real advantage of your own hand, a pair should never be laid out in the dealer's crib. "Touching cards," such as a 6 and a 7 or a 9 and a 10, are not proper cards for you to put in the dealer's crib because they are too likely to result in sequences when combined with the dealer's lay-out cards and the turn-up card. You should not lay out two cards of the same suit if you can equally well lay out cards of different suits and thus prevent a flush in the crib.

The best single cards to discard in the dealer's crib are a King and an Ace. They are least likely to be of value in making up a sequence, because a sequence can only be made on one side of them. A sequence can be made on both sides of cards of any other rank. On the other hand, an Ace is often a good card to retain in the hand because of its value in the hand or in pegging to make up a 15 or a 31 when combined with 6's, 7's, and 8's, or with 4's and tenth cards.

In general, the safest cards to lay out in the dealer's crib are cards which are widely separated in rank such as a King and an 8, a Queen and a 7, or a 9 and a 2. These are cards that cannot be united by the other cards in the crib to form a sequence. However, remember that any two cards you lay out in the crib, no matter how far apart in rank they may be, when combined with the dealer's layout cards and the turn-up card can produce a crib with a high count.

It is not good policy to lay out a Jack in the dealer's crib if you can avoid doing so. Besides being one of the sixteen tenth cards that can combine with 5's (or cards adding up to 5) to make 15, a Jack of the same suit as the turn-up card adds 1 point to the value of your hand. While the odds are three to one against this happening, you still have a chance and every point counts.

If you are within sight of game and have sufficient count in your hand to put you out, what you lay out in the dealer's crib becomes unimportant. On the other hand, if you are behind in the game and hold a double run as well as two other cards that make a 15, or make a pair, even if they are a pair of 5's, it would be to your advantage to put them in the dealer's crib and retain your double run. The odds in favour of your hand being improved in value by the turn-up card are worth the risk, and there are many occasions when even a pair of 5's do not materially add to the value of the crib.

Sample Hands for Laying Away   Suppose a hand contains Q, 9, 7, 6, 4, 2. Either player should keep 9, 6, 4, and 2, which count 4 points. These are good pegging cards, and offer many possibilities for materially improving the final count of the hand through the turn-up card, as shown in the following table.

9 as turn-up card will bring count up to 10
6 as turn-up card will bring count up to 8
4 as turn-up card will bring count up to 8
2 as turn-up card will bring count up to 8
3 as turn-up card will bring count up to 9
5 as turn-up card will bring count up to 9
7 as turn-up card will bring count up to 6

The Q and 7 may not be as good as you would like for your own crib, but on the other hand they are not much good to your opponent if the crib is his. These two cards are wide apart in rank and the chances are that they will not contribute much to building up the count of the crib.

Suppose the hand contains K, 8, 8, 6, 5, 3. In this case the situation is somewhat different. The non-dealer should lay away the K and 3. The dealer should lay away the two 8's. To the experienced player the reasons are obvious, but they may not be so clear to the novice.

The non-dealer by laying away the K and 3 has contributed to his opponent's crib two cards that are wide apart in rank and offer little opportunity for combining with other cards to produce a crib with substantial score. By holding the 8, 8, 6, 5, he has a count of only 2 but has many chances to peg as well as to improve the count of his hand with the turn-up card. The following table shows the possibilities of improving the count of the hand through the turn-up card.

2 as turn-up card will bring count up to 6
4 as turn-up card will bring count up to 7
5 as turn-up card will bring count up to 4
6 as turn-up card will bring count up to 4
7 as turn-up card will bring count up to 14
8 as turn-up card will bring count up to 6
9 as turn-up card will bring count up to 4
10, J, Q, or K as turn-up card will bring count up to 4

The dealer by laying away the pair of 8's has provided the crib with a pair of cards which offer excellent opportunities for a substantial count in the crib. By retaining K, 6, 5, 3, the dealer's hand, even though it contains a count of only 2, offers good opportunities for pegging, as well as for improved value when combined with the turn-up card:

2 as turn-up card will bring count up to 4
3 as turn-up card will bring count up to 4
4 as turn-up card will bring count up to 8
5 as turn-up card will bring count up to 6
6 as turn-up card will bring count up to 6
7 as turn-up card will bring count up to 7
9 as turn-up card will bring count up to 4
10, J, or Q as turn-up card will bring count up to 4
K as turn-up card will bring count up to 6

Here is another example. Suppose the hand contains J, 8, 5, 3, 3, A. This hand is somewhat more complicated, in that two different opportunities are provided to hold a count of 4—J, 5, 3, 3 and 8, 3, 3, A. Both appear equally attractive from the point of view of pegging. Both offer good possibilities for improvement in count through the turn-up card:

J, 5, 3, 3, with

      2 as turn-up card will have a count of 8
      3 as turn-up card will have a count of 8
      4 as turn-up card will have a count of 12
      7 as turn-up card will have a count of 8
      9 as turn-up card will have a count of 6
10, Q, K as turn-up card will have a count of 6
      J as turn-up card will have a count of 8

8, 3, 3, A, with

      2 as turn-up card will have a count of 10
      3 as turn-up card will have a count of 14
      4 as turn-up card will have a count of 8
      6 as turn-up card will have a count of 6
      7 as turn-up card will have a count of 6
      8 as turn-up card will have a count of 8
      9 as turn-up card will have a count of 6

With the hands about equal, attention should be given to the two cards for the crib. They have become the factor on which to base the decision as to which hand should be held.

The dealer should lay away the J and 5 because they provide 2 points in his crib and they offer good chances for improvement in the crib count through the discards of his opponent as well as through the turn-up card.

The non-dealer should lay away the 8 and A because they are wide apart in rank and tend to balk the dealer through providing fewer opportunities for increasing the count in the crib.

One more example—9, 7, 4, 3, 2, A.

The non-dealer should lay away the 7 and A. The dealer should lay away the 9 and 7.

By laying away the 7 and A, the non-dealer retains a count of 5 in his hand, with good possibilities of further improving it with the turn-up card. At the same time, the 7 and A laid away tend to balk his opponent in the crib because they are quite widely separated in rank.

By laying away the 9 and 7 the dealer has made a contribution to the crib that offers possibilities for improving the count because they are close in rank. By retaining 4, 3, 2, and A, a count of 4 is assured and many opportunities for improvement are possible with the turn-up card. The hand also offers excellent opportunities for pegging.

The cards you lay away in the crib (yours or your opponent's), the cards you retain in your hand, and the sequence in which you play those

cards during the progress of the game are all factors which are governed to a degree by your position in the game. If you are in reach of game, this
too has an effect which must be carefully considered.

Chapter V

Other Cribbage Games

Three-hand Cribbage

The rules of play and scoring are in general the same as in two-hand, six-card cribbage.

The cards are cut by all three players to determine which player has the first deal. Low card wins the deal.

Five cards are dealt separately and in rotation, clockwise, to each player. After the fifteenth card has been dealt, a sixteenth card is laid face down on the table in front of the dealer to make the foundation for the crib. To this card each of the three players adds one card from his hand. These four cards constitute the crib.

Each player has four cards left in his hand. The player to the left of the dealer makes the cut for the starter and plays first. The play then follows in clockwise rotation. The deal also follows in clockwise rotation from player to player. The hands are counted in the same rotation and order, beginning with the player on the left of the dealer. The dealer counts his hand and crib last.

Most modern cribbage boards have three parallel rows of holes so that one row can be used by each player. However, the game can be played on boards with only two rows of holes, provided each player can readily identify his own pegs. Usually when playing on a board of this type, the third player finds it necessary to move his pegs from side to side or row to row to avoid conflict with the pegs of an opponent. It is a little awkward, but it can be done.

In this game, all three players are independent, so you have two opponents instead of one. Should you be leading in the game, you can expect your two opponents to combine their efforts to balk you and, at the same time, improve their own positions even though they must favour each other to do so.

You will be about even if you win one game out of three, since you get a double stake, furnished by the two losers, when you win.

It is an interesting game that requires careful and ingenious play if you are to keep even.

In three-hand cribbage the count of the average hand is slightly less than in the four-hand game, averaging slightly more than seven. On the other hand, the crib will average almost five which is somewhat more than in the four-hand game.

Four-hand Cribbage

Again, the rules of play and scoring are in general the same as in two-hand, six-card cribbage.

The game is played by four persons in two pairs of partners. Unless it has been previously agreed who shall be partners, the game should commence by all four players cutting to determine partners and who shall have the first deal. Then each pair of partners should determine which of them shall have the management of the scoring. The board is then placed between these two opponents and they are the only two players who are permitted to touch the pegs and attend to the scoring. However, the other two players may prompt their partners and point out any omissions or errors they observe. Because of their common interest, partners may assist each other in counting the value of their hands and cribs.

As in three-hand cribbage, the deal and crib rotate in clockwise rotation from player to player.

43

Five cards are dealt separately and in rotation to each player. Each player lays away one card in the crib. The player to the left of the dealer makes the cut for the starter and plays first. The play then follows in clockwise rotation.

Remember that it is to your advantage to favour your own crib and that of your partner, and you lay away the worst cards in your opponent's crib. A 5 is an excellent card to put in your own crib, but a dangerous one to lay away in an opponent's crib. Aces and other small cards are usually good to hold in the hand because of the opportunities they provide to gain points in pegging a 15, a Go, or a 31. Tenth cards are usually good cards to contribute to an opponent's crib.

The player on the dealer's left plays first and the play then follows clockwise round the table until all of the sixteen cards have been played. The scoring and counting is done in the same manner as in six-card cribbage. The strategy is much the same too, but the playing out of each hand requires greater watchfulness and skill if partners are to gain the maximum from the cards in their hands.

A 5 is perhaps the worst card to lead because of the sixteen chances it gives your opponent to play a tenth card for a 15 and 2 points. A 9 is also a bad lead because if your opponent plays a 6 for a 15 and 2 points, your partner, if he pairs the 6, makes the count 21, which offers too many chances to your opponents for a 31 and 2 points. Similarly, an Ace is a poor lead because your opponent may then play a tenth card, making the count 11. Then should your partner pair that tenth card for 2 points, he would make the count 21, and again offer too many chances to the next opponent to gain 31 for 2 points, or 8 points (6 for pairs royal and 2 for 31) if he can again pair that tenth card.

One point should be made clear; any cards that can "come in" under 31 must be played. Suppose in the play of a hand you have just played a card to make the count 27. The following player says "Go," your partner says "Go," and so does the next player. The turn has again come to you and you still hold a pair of 2's. You must play them, saying "29" as you play the first and "31 for 4 points" as you play the second.

When it seems certain that the game will be reached through pegging during the course of play, you should keep in your hand those cards which are best for pegging regardless of what card you are forced to put in the crib.

After the sixteen cards have been played out, the hands will be counted beginning with the player on the left of the dealer and following clockwise round the table. The dealer counts his hand and crib last.

45

In this game, the average count of each hand should be about 7, while the crib should yield between 4 and 5.

Five Card Cribbage
(The Original Game)

At the outset the two players cut for deal. The player cutting the highest card wins the deal. The player who loses the deal pegs 3 holes to compensate him for the advantage which his opponent has in having the first crib.

Five cards are dealt, one at a time, face down, alternately to each player. The balance of the pack is then placed, face down, on the table. Each player lays down two cards for the crib. The dealer's opponent then cuts the remainder of the pack and the dealer turns up the top card.

The method of play is generally the same as for the six-card game, but with this important exception: play stops when the first Go or 31 has been reached.

Should the play stop with a Go, the player who played the last card scores 1 for the Go. Should the play stop with a 31, the player who played the last card to make the count 31 scores 2.

The dealer's opponent counts his hand first and then the dealer counts his hand and crib.

The counting of the hands and crib is similar to

46

the counting of the six-card game. However, the value of the hands will be considerably lower because only four cards are involved. On the other hand, the crib will average about the same as in the six-card game (because five cards are included).

In this game, if a player holds three cards of the same suit in his hand, he counts 3 for the flush. If the starter or turn-up card is also of the same suit, he counts 4. To have a flush in the crib, all five cards must be of the same suit, just as in the six-card game.

The game is set at 61 points. If "lurch" or "skunk" has been agreed upon, one player must gain 61 points before the other has reached 31, and a game thus won counts as two.

Chapter VI

Statistics and Odds

The element of chance in cribbage governs the deal and the value of the starter card, but the actual count of the hand is considerably influenced by the skill of the player in choosing which cards to hold and which to consign to the crib.

Both here and in the play of the cards some knowledge of probabilities is helpful. Many deals present the player with difficult choices. Sometimes there is an embarrassment of riches (A, 2, 3, 3, 4, 4) and it is impossible to discard to the crib without a painful reduction in the count held. At other times one is faced with a scattered collection which must depend on the starter card for any hope of a decent count.

It is easy to agonize over such situations, but quite profitless. One wants to maximize the chance of a good count. This can always be done with a knowledge of the probabilities. The tables on pages 75 to 98 are intended to show what is involved in certain types of hand, and the method of presentation indicates a procedure by which any given case may be analyzed.

However, it would be misleading to suggest that a mathematical approach to the game gives a sure and sufficient foundation for expertise. This is far from the case. If one always does the logical thing in a game, one's play becomes too predictable; opponents catch on and shape their tactics accordingly.

Probability is a measure of the likelihood that a given event will occur. If we consider some unspecified event A, which can occur in m ways and not occur in n ways, and if all these ways are *equally likely*, then the probability of the event occurring is

$$\frac{m}{m+n}$$

and the probability that it will not occur is

$$\frac{n}{m+n}$$

The total probability that the event will occur or

not occur is obtained by addition of the above fractions:

$$\frac{m+n}{m+n} = 1$$

Thus a probability of 1 indicates a certainty. At the other end of the scale, 0 represents an impossibility. Between these two limits the larger the fraction the more probable the result.

For example, what is the probability of cutting a 7 from a full pack of cards? There are four ways in which the desired result may be achieved, and forty-eight in which it will fail. The probability is therefore four in fifty-two, or $\frac{1}{13}$.

If two events A and B are dependent, then the probability that they both will occur is the product of their individual probabilities. Consider, for instance, the probability of drawing two 4's in succession from a pack of cards, without having replaced the first 4. Event A, drawing the first 4, has a probability of $\frac{1}{13}$. For event B, the drawing of the second 4, there are three ways to succeed and still forty-eight ways to fail, giving a probability of $\frac{3}{51}$. The probability of drawing two 4's is therefore $\frac{1}{13} \times \frac{1}{17}$, or $\frac{1}{221}$.

If two events are independent the probability

that one *or* the other occurs is the sum of the individual probabilities.

The figures given by application of these rules are only valid if the assumptions on which they are based hold true. The chief assumption is that all possible results are equally likely. This assumption is invalid if any order or bias exists. It often does.

One familiar example is the tossing of a coin, which is supposed with equal likelihood to fall heads or tails. In practice, however, most coins have a bias, a slight preference for one face rather than the other. (The cause is probably lack of symmetry between the obverse and reverse designs.)

In cribbage, at least in some phases of the game, there is a much more pronounced bias. You may calculate elaborately how to hold for maximum count, assuming that the cards placed by the opponent in the crib are of random value and that no bonus or penalty need be assigned to one's own crib cards. But your opponent's choice will not be random; he will exhibit a remarkable bias against putting good cards in your crib, or bad ones in his own.

Nevertheless, the tables included here show most probable value of hand without considering the state of the crib, or the identity of the cards to be placed there. For this, the author must plead for compassion: to take statistical account of these factors would increase the tabulations more than three hundred-fold.

One other remark about the nature of probabilities may be appropriate. Any fraction calculated according to the rules above measures the likelihood of an event occurring in any given trial, and in addition the most probable number of occurrences in a long series of trials. One would expect a 7 to be cut four times in fifty-two trials. However, this is not a certainty, and in fact the possible results range from zero to fifty-two times. We have the paradox that the most probable result is actually quite improbable, and becomes more so as the chances become slimmer. We know that four cuts of a 7 in fifty-two tries is more probable than three or five, or any other of the fifty-two possible results. In all cases such as this, where the event is random, one can also calculate how much more probable is one result compared to another.

For a realistic example of the value and limitations of a statistical approach, let us turn now to one of the tense situations in the play of the cards. You are dealer in a two-handed game. Your opponent plays a Deuce. You hold a Deuce. The starter is not a Deuce. Do you pair for 2 points and accept the risk of pairs royal for 6?

Knowledge of your opponent's style of play is

by far the best basis for decision. Does he lead from a low pair every time he has one? But you may not possess the advantage of that priceless knowledge. Then you must rely on probabilities.

The identity of eight cards is known to you—the six dealt to you, the starter, and the Deuce played by your opponent. The other forty-four, containing two Deuces, are unknown. It can probably be assumed that your opponent did not split a pair in laying away for the crib, and therefore still holds all the Deuces he received in the deal.

What must be ascertained is the probability of whether none, one, or both of the missing Deuces were included in the five unknown cards dealt to your opponent.

Let us suppose that the five unknown cards were drawn one at a time from the pack of forty-four. There are forty-four ways in which the first one may be drawn, forty-three for the second, forty-two for the third, forty-one for the fourth and forty for the fifth.

If we first examine the case in which no Deuces are drawn, there are clearly forty-two ways to achieve this in the first draw, forty-one in the second, ranging down to thirty-eight in the fifth.

The probability for the draws is thus $\frac{42}{44}, \frac{41}{43}, \frac{40}{42}$, $\frac{39}{41}, \frac{38}{40}$ respectively. The five draws are dependent; that is to say, the probability assigned to the second depends on the result of the first, and so on. Therefore, using the first rule above, the probability is the product of the five fractions. These simplify conveniently to $\frac{1482}{1892}$.

The second case, in which one of the missing Deuces is contained in the opponent's five unknown cards, is calculated similarly. The chance that the first card of the five is a Deuce is $\frac{2}{44}$. The chances that the other four are not are $\frac{42}{43}, \frac{41}{42}, \frac{40}{41}$ and $\frac{39}{40}$ respectively.

The probability that only one Deuce was dealt, as the first of five cards, is therefore

$$\frac{2 \times 42 \times 41 \times 40 \times 39}{44 \quad 43 \quad 42 \quad 41 \quad 40} = \frac{2 \times 39}{44 \quad 43} = \frac{78}{1892}.$$

However, with equal likelihood the Deuce might have been received as the second, third, fourth, or fifth card. Thus the total probability of one Deuce and only one in the five cards is

$$\frac{5 \times 78}{1892} = \frac{390}{1892}$$

Finally we investigate the case of both missing Deuces being included in the five cards. The card-by-card probabilities are $\frac{2}{44}, \frac{1}{43}$, 1, 1, 1 respectively. Also there are ten ways in which the two

Deuces could have been received, of which the above case is one. (The ten ways are first and second, first and third, etc.)

The total probability of two Deuces is therefore

$$\frac{2 \times 10}{1892} = \frac{20}{1892}$$

As a check, we add the probabilities for each of the three cases

$$\frac{1482 + 390 + 20}{1892} = \frac{1892}{1892} = 1$$

Since one or other of the three cases *must* occur, the probabilities must total to unity, which they do.

The information so derived can be used to perform a cost-benefit analysis. Consider 1892 cases, in each of which you benefit by pairing to the extent of 2 points for a total benefit of 3784 points. In 1482 cases the opponent cannot score pairs royal and there is no penalty. In the remaining 410 cases he can do so, for a total cost of 2460 points.

Thus by pairing every time you accrue a net benefit of 1324 points, or very close to .7 points per pair.

It is hardly necessary to observe that this sort of calculation could not be made as occasion arises during the play of the cards. However the final figure of merit for pairing may well be remembered, and used (after tempering by other considerations) as need arises. There are many other considerations. For instance, can you play to 15, making 2 points, with less risk?

Also it will be obvious that the conditions assumed in this example are the most dangerous so far as pairs royal are concerned. The risk becomes smaller if the opponent has already played one or more cards, or if the starter card is of the same value as the card to be paired. Finally, the risk disappears completely if one holds a pair in one's own hand!

Therefore, in the absence of any other consideration, score the pair.

Another use for percentage play is apt to arise in selecting a hand after the deal, and it is here that the tables included in this book may be of assistance.

Suppose, for example, you are dealt 2, 4, 5, 6, 9, 10 in a two-handed game. What do you hold? The selections 4, 5, 6, 9, and 4, 5, 6, 10 both count 7. In either case, the crib cards are not too dangerous. Yet there is a difference. It is slightly better to hold the 4, 5, 6, 9. To see why, look in the table of three sequences on page 76. There the value added for each possible starter card is taken into account for the sequence 4, 5, 6 with either a 9 or a 10 completing the hand. In a long enough series of trials the holding 4, 5, 6, 9 is likely to have a final count of $9 \frac{41}{48}$ on the average, whereas the hand 4, 5, 6,

10 will average $9\frac{33}{48}$. There is not a great differ-ence, but eight points in forty-eight hands of this kind are not to be sneezed at.

There is a principle involved here which if rec-ognized will serve you better than constant re-course to tabulated statistics. If nothing else is in-volved, medium or smaller cards offer more possi-bilities for combining into 15's than do larger ones. Tenth cards are worst of all. However, Jacks are an exception because of their value when the starter is of the same suit.

The same principle may be seen in another sort of hand. Referring to the figures on pairs royal, it is observed that 6, 6, 6, 3 is apt to be a slightly bet-ter holding than 6, 6, 6, 9.

Again, the average potential value of 3, 4, 5, x (containing no 15's) is somewhat higher than the potential value of 9, 10, J, x.

From such small advantages, based on percent-age principles, a winning edge may often be de-veloped.

Chapter VII

Terms Used In Cribbage

Dealing   The cards are dealt one at a time, face down, beginning with the non-dealer. Each player receives six cards if two are playing; five cards if three or four are playing.

Bust Hand   A hand which contains no count.

Laying Away or Discarding   After examining his hand, each player lays away two cards face down. These four cards form the crib, which belongs to and counts for the dealer. If three or four are playing, each player lays away one card. If three are playing, one card is dealt to the crib by the dealer after he has dealt the five cards to each player.

The Starter or Turn-up Card After both players have laid away two cards for the crib, the non-dealer cuts the cards. The dealer turns up the top card of the lower pack and places it on top of the pack. (If this "starter" is a Jack, the dealer pegs 2 points.)

The Crib The four cards laid out by the players at the start of the game.

Salting the Crib Laying away cards in the crib that will be of the greatest possible advantage to the dealer.

Tenth Card Kings, Queens, Jacks, and tens all have the rank of ten in the play of the game and in the counting of the hands.

Pairs Two cards of the same rank, and similar. Each pair counts for 2 points. (Non-similar tenth cards do not constitute a pair.)

Pairs Royal or Three of a Kind or Triplets Three similar cards of the same rank. If held in the hand or crib they count for 6 points, because they are equivalent to three pairs. Here is an example—

59

place the 4 of Diamonds, the 4 of Spades, and the 4 of Clubs face up on the table. The 4 of Diamonds and the 4 of Spades form a pair; the 4 of Diamonds and the 4 of Clubs form a second pair; the 4 of Spades and the 4 of Clubs form a third. By the same token, if you hold in your hand or crib a pair of 4's and the starter or turn-up card is a 4, you would again count 6 points.

Further, should they follow in order during the play of the game, the one who plays the third 4 scores 6 points; provided of course that the total does not exceed 31. Suppose the non-dealer starts the play with a 4. The dealer then plays the second 4 and says "8, and 2 points for the pair" and pegs 2 holes. If the non-dealer has another 4, he will play it and say "12, and 6 points for pairs royal (or triplets)." He would then peg the 6 points.

The same scoring applies to tenth cards only if they are similar, such as three Jacks or three Kings.

Double Pairs Royal or Double Pairs or Four of a Kind   Four similar cards of the same rank. If held in the hand or crib (including the starter) they count for 12 points, because they are equivalent to six pairs. To demonstrate double pairs royal, lay out all four 4's face up on the table.

4D 4S 4C 4H

4D and 4S make a pair for 2 points   2

4D and 4C make a second pair for 2 points 2

4D and 4H make a third pair for 2 points   2

4S and 4C make a fourth pair for 2 points   2

4S and 4H make a fifth pair for 2 points   2

4C and 4H make a sixth pair for 2 points   2

<u>12</u> Total

Or, as in pairs royal, should they follow in order during the play of the game, the one who plays the fourth 4 scores 12 points (provided, of course, that the total does not exceed 31).

Of course, this scoring applies only to cards having a rank of 7 or less, because four cards of higher rank could not come in under 31.

15's   Every combination of 15 counts for 2 points, whether the 15 is made during the play of the game or in the counting of the hands or crib. (This applies whether the 15 is made with two cards, such as a 9 and a 6, or a 10 and a 5, or by three or more cards, an 8, 2, 5 or a 3, 4, 8, etc.)

Sequences or Runs   Three, four, or more cards of successive rank, whether of the same suit or otherwise, count for as many points as there are cards in the sequence. This applies to sequences made during the play or to those held in the hand or crib.

Play on   To play the card that makes a sequence or run, or makes one possible with the play of further cards.

Play off   To play a card of wide difference in rank and thus prevent a run or sequence.

Flush   The four cards in your hand being all of one suit is a flush, and counts 4. If the starter or turn-up card is of the same suit, the total count is 5. Four cards of the same suit in the crib do not count unless the starter is also of the same suit. The count is then 5.

A flush cannot be made during the play. It can only occur in the count of the hands or crib.

31   Every time a player makes exactly 31 points in the course of play, he scores 2 points. In scoring the hands or crib, a 31 has no value.

Go   If neither player can play a card to make exactly 31, the one who plays the last card making the number nearest to but less than 31, scores 1 point for the "Go."

Last Card   The player who plays the last card in the play after each deal scores 1 point. The only occasion when this 1 point is not allowed is when the play of the last card makes a 31. This entitles the player of the last card to 2 points for the 31, but not to an additional point for last card.

His Nob or His Nibs   If the starter is a Jack, the dealer pegs 2 points for "His Nob." Should either player hold in his hand, or the crib, the Jack of the same suit as the starter, he pegs 1 point for "His Nob."

Game Hole   The 121st hole, or end of the game.

Mud Hole   The 120th hole.

Counting Out   Near the end of the game, if the non-dealer has sufficient points in his hand he may "count out" to win the game before the dealer has a chance to count.

The Lurch or Skunk   Most modern cribbage boards which have 121 holes in a continuous line have the "lurch" or "skunk" line marked between the 90th and 91st hole. "Lurch" or "Skunk" does not apply unless agreed upon at the start of the game. In that case, it counts as a double game if one player pegs 121 points before his opponent has pegged 91.

The Double Skunk   The double skunk line is drawn between the 60th and 61st holes. If one player pegs 121 points before his opponent has pegged 61, it counts as four games.

Muggins   This is optional and to apply it should be agreed upon at the start of the game. Each player must count his own hand (and crib) aloud and announce the total. Should he overlook any score, his opponent may say "Muggins" and then himself score the points overlooked.

Game   The game may be fixed at 61 points but is normally 121 points. The play ends, and no further counting can be done by either player, at the moment either player reaches the agreed total, whether he reaches it by pegging or by counting his hand.

Chapter VIII

The Rules of Cribbage

1. Before the start of each game, the cards must be cut to determine who the dealer shall be. When rubbers are being played, the starting deal for each game alternates.
2. When cutting for deal, the first to cut should remove at least the top four cards; but he should not remove more than half the pack, so that a suitable number of cards remains for the player who cuts last.
3. The player who cuts the highest card wins the cut and has first deal. (Note: In many places modern usage has altered this rule and,

through local custom, the *lowest* card wins the cut and first deal.) Should the players draw cards of the same rank, they must draw again.

4. All players have the right to shuffle the cards, but the dealer has the right to do so last.

5. The cards must be dealt out one by one, the first card going to the dealer's opponent, the next to the dealer, and alternating until the deal is completed.

6. If, during the course of the deal, the dealer exposes one of his own cards, no penalty is invoked; but if he exposes one of his opponent's cards, the opponent scores 2 points and may, in addition, demand a new deal, provided he does so before looking at the rest of his cards.

7. Should the opponent expose one of his cards before the deal is completed, the dealer has the choice of dealing over again provided he has not looked at his own hand.

8. Should a misdeal occur without the dealer being aware of it until one or both of the hands has been taken up, the opponent shall score 2 points and the cards must be shuffled and dealt again.

9. Should the dealer give his opponent more than the proper number of cards, there must be a new deal and the opponent scores 2 points,

provided the error is discovered before the opponent picks up his cards. If the error is not discovered until after the opponent has picked up his cards, he cannot score the 2 points, but there must be a new deal.

10. Should the dealer give to himself more than the proper number of cards, the opponent may call for a new deal or draw the extra card or cards from the hand of the dealer.

11. Should the dealer give either player (but not both) fewer than the proper number of cards, there must be a new deal.

12. Should the dealer deal two cards at once to either player, there must be a new deal unless the opponent agrees to have the surplus card withdrawn and placed on top of the pack.

13. If, following the deal and the picking up of the cards, either player finds either more or fewer than the proper number of cards in the hand of his opponent, he scores 2 points and calls for a new deal.

NOTE: The proper number of cards depends upon the particular type of cribbage being played. In six-card cribbage with two players, the proper number of cards is six. The same game with either three or four players is played with five cards. Five cards are also used in the original five-card game with two players.

14. At the commencement of the game the players must decide whether the "lurch" or "skunk" shall apply. If it is agreed to, the game counts double if one player scores 121 points before his opponent has scored 91. If the double "lurch" or "skunk" is to apply, the game counts as four games if one player scores 121 before his opponent scores 61.

15. When the deal has been completed, the pack that was dealt from shall not be touched by any player until the time has come to cut for the "start" of play. Should a player touch the deck, the opposing player scores 2 points.

16. The opponent must discard for the crib first. He discards two cards, if six-card cribbage is being played with two players, to reduce his hand to four (one card if either three or four players are in the game). The dealer then follows with his discards. A card once placed in the crib cannot be taken up again. The crib belongs to the dealer, but it is not exposed or used until after the play is completed.

17. Should either player confuse his cards with the crib, the other player scores 3 points and calls for a new deal.

18. Only the dealer is entitled to touch the crib, but he may not do so until the play of the hand is completed and he takes up the crib to count it.

19. When the opponent is cutting for the "start" of play, he must remove at least three cards from the top of the deck, and he must leave at least four cards on the bottom. The dealer then turns up the top card of the lower packet. This card is then placed, face up, on the top of the pack.

    NOTE: Many players when cutting for the "start" lift the packet of cards and look at the card on the bottom of the packet they have removed, or make it possible for their opponent to see it. This practice is not permitted in any card game where a "cut" is involved. It should not be permitted in cribbage because it could provide an unfair advantage to the player or players who know the rank of that bottom card.

20. When the cut for the "start" has been made, if the turn-up card is a Jack, the dealer is entitled to score 2 points for "His Nob." (The expression "two for His Nob." came from "Knoddy," an earlier game from which cribbage may have developed.)

    NOTE: Some players have the mistaken idea that the dealer may not score the 2 points if he is within 6 points of game. This is not so. He scores the 2 points even if by so doing he reaches 121 points or game.

21. The dealer must score the 2 points for "His

Nob" before he has played his first card or he forfeits the 2 points. (It is important to note that he may score the 2 points even though his opponent has played his first card.)

22. Should a player take, or peg, more points than he is entitled to when scoring for a penalty or when counting his hand or crib, he may be set back the number of points he has over-scored so that the scoring is corrected. In addition, his adversary adds the same number of points to his own score.

23. Should a player neglect to score points to which he is entitled as the result of a penalty or when counting his hand or crib, there is no penalty unless it has been agreed in advance that "Muggins" will apply. In that case, the opposing player may say "Muggins" and then himself score the points overlooked.

24. Should a player touch the pegs of his adversary except to correct an error in score, or should he touch his own pegs except when he has a right to score, he shall forfeit 2 points to his opponent.

25. Should both pegs of a player be displaced by accident, the opponent must be allowed to restore them to their places. Should the player refuse this right to his opponent, then the opponent may claim the game.

26. Should only the foremost peg be displaced by

accident it must be put back to the hole behind the back peg of the player to whom it belongs.

NOTE: Modern practice disregards this rule and allows the peg to be put back in the hole from which it was displaced, or if there is uncertainty as to the hole from which it was displaced, the peg is put back in a hole agreed upon by both players.

27. Once the pegs have been quitted by a player when scoring points, the score cannot be altered.

28. Should a player neglect to mark his score for either his hand or crib before putting the cards away in the deck, he forfeits the points he might have claimed.

29. Should a card that may legally be played be "shown" by putting it on the board, it cannot be reclaimed.

30. Should a card be "shown" that cannot legally be played according to the rules of the game, it can be reclaimed by the erring player without any penalty ensuing.

31. Should a player neglect to play when he could have "come in" under 31, his opponent may score 2 points.

32. Should either player call a number in mistake during the progress of the game, there is no penalty.

33. Should a player, in error, score a game as won that he has not won, he forfeits the game.

34. The hand and crib must be laid out plainly when counting and must remain so until the opponent understands the count being claimed for it.

35. When counting a hand or crib, each player must determine his own count and announce the total aloud. He cannot seek the assistance of his opponent. In four-hand cribbage, however, he may ask and receive the assistance of his partner.

36. Should a player refuse to pay any penalty he may have incurred by infringing the rules of play, his opponent may claim the game.

37. Spectators of the game shall not in any way assist either player or interfere in any way with the progress of the game.

Chapter IX

Tables

Average Value Added

The method of calculating "average value added" is illustrated in the following example. The cards held in hand are assumed to be A, 2, 3, 5, having a count of three.

If the starter is: A 2 3 4 5 6 7 8 9 10 J Q K
The value added is: 5 5 5 4 4 2 4 2 4 4 4 4 4
The ways in which each possible
starter may be cut are: 3 3 3 4 3 4 4 4 4 4 4 4 4
The total of the bottom line is forty-eight, representing the total number of ways in which a

73

starter may be cut. Actually there are not forty-eight cards present when the cut is made. This need not concern us, because the opponent's hand and crib cards are not specified. Their selection from the pack was random and may be disregarded for our purpose here. Our assumption does not give the correct answer for any given deal, but it does give the result to be expected over a long series of like deals.

We consider a series of forty-eight deals, in which each possible starter is cut once. The total value added is obtained by multiplying each value in the second line with the number of ways shown directly below it, and then summing all the products. The answer in this case is 185 points.

Dividing by forty-eight gives the "average value added" for a single hand, and this is the value shown in the tables. Note that it is in most cases impossible to have the average value added in any single hand! The "average total count" is the sum of the count originally held and the average value added.

The tables include a few of the most interesting types of hand, but only a tiny fraction of all possible hands. By using the method described here, the reader may analyze any case of interest to him.

Jacks

Adjustment for Jacks held in hand has been made as follows:

If one Jack is held, it will count one if a card of the same suit is cut as starter. There are 12 ways of doing this out of fifty-one cards unspecified as to suit. The probability is thus 12/51, and the average value added on account of the Jack is 12/51 points. In the case of two, three, or four Jacks the values by similar reasoning are 24/50, 36/49 and 48/48.

These have been rounded for the sake of arithmetic convenience.   The values used in the tables are thus eleven, twenty-three, thirty-five, and forty-eight forty-eighths respectively.

Flushes

No account has been taken of flushes. In hands where these are possible, the average value added is by reasoning similar to that used in the case of Jacks, 4 9/48 in the case where only four of a suit are held before discarding.

SEQUENCE OF THREE

Value Held	Cards Held	If Starter is: A	2	3	4	5	6	7	8	9	10	J	Q	K	Average Value added is: Units	48ths	Average Total Count Units	48ths
		value added is:																
3	A 2 3 5	5	5	5	4	4	2	4	2	4	4	4	4	4	3	41	6	41
3	A 2 3 6	5	5	7	3	2	6	2	2	4	2	2	2	2	3	9	6	9
3	A 2 3 7	5	7	7	3	4	2	4	2	2	2	2	2	2	3	9	6	9
3	A 2 3 8	7	7	7	5	2	2	2	2	2	2	2	2	2	3	9	6	9
5	A 2 3 9	7	7	9	3	2	0	0	4	2	2	2	2	2	2	45	7	45
5	A 2 3 10	7	9	7	3	2	0	0	0	2	4	2	2	2	2	37	7	37
5	A 2 3 J	7	9	7	3	2	0	0	0	2	2	4	2	2	3	0	8	0
5	A 2 3 Q	7	9	7	3	2	0	0	0	2	2	2	4	2	2	37	7	37
5	A 2 3 K	7	9	7	3	2	0	0	0	2	2	2	2	4	2	37	7	37
5	2 3 4 6	1	7	7	7	4	6	2	2	2	2	2	2	2	3	21	8	21
3	7	3	7	7	7	3	4	2	4	2	2	2	2	2	3	21	6	21
5	8	3	7	7	7	3	2	2	4	2	2	2	2	2	3	11	8	11
5	9	3	7	7	7	1	4	0	2	4	2	2	2	2	3	3	8	3
5	10	3	7	7	5	3	2	0	2	2	4	2	2	2	2	45	7	45
5	J	3	7	7	5	3	2	0	2	2	2	4	2	2	3	8	8	8

5		Q/K	37753202	2422	2	45	7	45
3	3	A	24754222	4444	4	3	7	3
5	4	7	21975440	2222	3	13	8	13
5		8	03973440	2222	3	3	8	3
3		9	23955220	2222	3	7	6	7
5		10	23757220	2224	2	45	7	45
5		J	23757720	2242	3	8	8	8
5		Q/K	23757320	2422	2	45	7	45
5	4	A	20397124	4444	3	41	8	41
5	5	2	04497324	2222	3	21	8	21
5		8	22377422	2222	3	9	8	9
7		9	22179104	2222	2	41	9	41
7		10	20179102	2222	2	33	9	33
7		J	20179710	2244	2	44	9	44
7		Q/K	20179710	2422	2	43	9	33
3	5	A	44355754	2422	3	31	6	31
5	6	2	24235752	2222	3	13	8	13
5	7	3	22447732	2222	3	15	8	15
5		9	22235553	2222	3	3	8	3

SEQUENCE OF THREE (Continued)

Value Held	Cards Held	If Starter is: value added is:													Average Value added is:		Average Total Count	
		A	2	3	4	5	6	7	8	9	10	J	Q	K	Units	48ths	Units	48ths
5	10	0	2	2	3	7	5	5	3	2	4	2	2	2	2	39	7	39
5	J	0	2	2	3	7	5	5	3	2	2	4	2	2	3	2	8	2
5	Q/K	0	2	2	3	7	5	5	3	2	2	2	4	2	2	39	7	39
7	6 7 8 A	6	2	0	0	1	7	9	9	3	0	0	0	0	2	21	9	21
7	2	2	4	0	0	3	7	9	7	3	0	0	0	0	2	17	9	17
5	3	2	2	2	2	3	7	7	7	3	0	0	0	0	2	21	7	21
5	4	2	2	2	4	4	5	7	7	3	0	0	0	0	2	25	7	25
5	10	2	2	0	0	3	5	7	7	4	2	0	0	0	2	11	7	11
5	J	2	2	0	0	3	5	7	7	3	0	2	0	0	2	18	7	18
5	Q/K	2	2	0	0	3	5	7	7	3	0	0	2	0	2	7	7	7
5	7 8 9 A	2	0	0	0	2	5	9	7	5	1	0	0	0	2	5	7	5
5	2	0	2	0	2	2	5	7	7	5	1	0	0	0	2	7	7	7
5	3	0	0	4	2	2	3	7	7	5	1	0	0	0	2	5	7	5
5	4	0	2	2	4	0	3	7	7	5	1	0	0	0	2	5	7	5
5	5	2	2	2	0	2	4	7	7	5	3	2	2	2	2	43	7	43

5	J	0 0 0 0 2 3 7 7 5	2 2 0 0	2	6	7	6
5	Q/K	0 0 0 0 2 3 7 7 5	1 0 2 0	1	39	6	39
3	8 9 10 A	2 0 0 2 4 4 3 5 5	5 1 0 0	2	11	5	11
3	2	0 2 2 2 4 2 3 5 5	5 1 0 0	2	11	5	11
3	3	2 2 4 2 2 2 3 5 5	5 1 0 0	2	9	5	9
3	4	2 2 2 2 2 2 3 5 5	5 1 0 0	2	11	5	11
5	5	2 2 0 0 4 2 3 5 5	7 3 2 2	2	31	7	31
5	6	2 0 0 0 2 4 4 5 7	5 1 0 0	2	3	7	3
3	Q	0 0 0 0 4 2 3 5 5	5 2 2 0	1	47	4	47
3	K	0 0 0 0 4 2 3 5 5	5 1 0 2	1	43	4	43
3	9 10 J A	2 0 0 4 6 2 0 1 5	5 5 1 0	2	22	5	22
3	2	0 2 4 2 4 2 0 1 5	5 5 1 0	2	22	5	22
3	3	0 4 4 0 4 2 0 1 5	5 5 1 0	2	20	5	20
3	4	4 2 0 2 4 2 0 1 5	5 5 1 0	2	22	5	22
7	5	2 0 0 0 6 2 0 1 5	7 7 3 2	2	30	9	30
5	6	0 0 0 0 4 4 0 1 7	5 5 1 0	2	2	7	2
3	7	0 0 0 0 4 2 2 4 5	5 5 1 0	2	10	5	10
3	K	0 0 0 0 6 2 0 1 5	5 5 2 2	2	10	5	10
3	10 J Q A	2 0 0 6 6 0 0 0 1	5 5 5 1	2	22	5	22
3	2	0 2 6 0 6 0 0 0 1	5 5 5 1	2	22	5	22

SEQUENCE OF THREE (Continued)

Value Held	Cards Held	A	2	3	4	5	6	7	8	9	10	J	Q	K	Average Value added is: Units	48ths	Average Total Count Units	48ths
3	3	0	6	2	0	6	0	0	0	1	5	5	5	1	2	22	5	22
3	4	6	0	0	2	6	0	0	0	1	5	5	5	1	2	22	5	22
9	5	0	0	0	8	0	0	0	1	7	7	7	3		2	18	11	18
3	6	0	0	0	0	6	2	0	0	3	5	5	5	1	2	6	5	6
3	7	0	0	0	0	6	0	2	2	1	5	5	5	1	2	6	5	6
3	8	0	0	0	0	6	0	2	2	2	5	5	5	1	2	10	5	10
3	J Q K A	2	0	0	6	6	0	0	0	0	1	5	5	5	2	18	5	18
3	2	0	2	6	0	6	0	0	0	0	1	5	5	5	2	18	5	18
3	3	0	6	2	0	6	0	0	0	0	1	5	5	5	2	18	5	18
3	4	6	0	0	2	6	0	0	0	0	1	5	5	5	2	18	5	18
9	5	0	0	0	8	0	0	0	0	0	3	7	7	7	2	14	11	14
3	6	0	0	0	6	2	0	0	0	2	1	5	5	5	2	2	5	2
3	7	0	0	0	6	0	2	2	0	0	1	5	5	5	2	2	5	2
3	8	0	0	0	6	0	2	2	0	0	1	5	5	5	2	2	5	2
3	9	0	0	0	6	2	0	0	0	2	2	5	5	5	2	6	5	6

STRAIGHTS

Value Held	Cards Held	If Starter is: A	2	3	4	5	6	7	8	9	10	J	Q	K	Average Val. added is: Units	48ths	Average Total Count Units	48ths
		value added is:																
4	A 2 3 4	6	6	6	6	3	2	2	4	4	4	4	4	4	4	4	8	4
4	2 3 4 5	3	6	8	8	8	5	2	4	2	4	4	4	4	4	26	8	26
6	3 4 5 6	2	3	8	8	8	10	3	2	2	2	2	2	2	3	38	9	38
6	4 5 6 7	0	2	3	10	8	8	6	3	2	2	2	2	2	3	24	9	24
6	5 6 7 8	2	4	2	3	6	6	8	8	3	2	2	2	2	3	28	9	28
8	6 7 8 9	2	2	0	0	0	1	8	8	8	1	0	0	0	2	24	10	24
6	7 8 9 10	0	0	0	0	2	8	8	8	8	6	1	0	0	2	12	8	12
4	8 9 10 J	0	0	0	0	4	3	6	6	6	6	6	1	0	2	27	6	27
4	9 10 J Q	0	0	0	0	6	2	0	1	6	6	6	6	1	2	27	6	27
4	10 J Q K	0	0	0	0	8	0	0	0	1	6	6	6	6	2	23	6	23

DOUBLE RUNS

Value Held	Cards Held				If Starter is: value added is: A	2	3	4	5	6	7	8	9	10	J	Q	K	Average Val. added is: Units	48ths	Average Total Count Units	48ths
8	A	A	2	3	7	8	8	2	0	0	0	2	4	4	4	4	4	3	14	11	14
8	A	2	2	3	8	7	8	2	0	0	2	2	4	6	6	6	6	4	6	12	6
8	A	2	3	3	8	8	7	2	0	2	2	2	6	4	4	4	4	3	38	11	38
8	2	2	3	4	2	7	8	10	2	4	2	4	4	4	4	4	4	4	12	12	12
8	2	3	3	4	2	8	9	8	4	4	4	4	4	4	4	4	4	4	18	12	18
8	2	3	4	4	2	10	8	9	4	4	2	4	4	2	2	2	2	3	40	11	40
10	3	3	4	5	0	2	11	10	4	4	4	4	2	2	2	2	2	3	34	13	34
8	3	4	4	5	0	4	12	9	8	6	4	4	0	2	2	2	2	3	38	11	38
8	3	4	5	5	2	4	12	8	9	6	4	4	2	0	4	4	4	4	22	12	22
12	4	4	5	6	2	2	2	9	12	12	4	0	2	2	2	2	2	3	26	15	26
12	4	5	5	6	2	0	2	12	11	12	2	0	2	2	4	4	4	3	46	15	46
12	4	5	6	6	0	0	4	12	12	9	2	0	4	2	2	2	2	3	18	15	18
8	5	5	6	7	0	2	4	6	9	8	8	4	2	4	4	4	4	4	10	12	10
8	5	6	6	7	0	4	4	6	8	7	8	4	4	2	2	2	2	3	38	11	38
8	5	6	7	7	2	4	4	4	8	8	7	6	2	2	2	2	2	3	38	11	38

2	38	30	14	6	10	14	14	14	25	25	37	25	37	25	29	17	17
13	14	14	14	14	12	10	10	10	10	10	10	10	10	10	10	10	10
2	38	30	14	6	10	14	14	14	25	25	37	25	37	25	29	17	17
3	2	2	2	2	2	2	2	2	2	2	2	2	2	2	2	2	2
0	0	0	0	0	0	0	0	0	0	0	0	2	2	2	8	8	7
0	0	0	0	0	0	0	0	0	2	2	2	8	8	7	8	7	8
0	0	0	0	0	0	2	2	2	8	8	7	8	7	8	7	8	8
0	0	0	2	2	2	8	8	7	8	7	8	7	8	8	2	2	2
6	4	4	8	8	7	8	7	8	7	8	8	2	2	2	0	0	0
10	10	12	9	12	9	12	7	8	8	2	2	2	0	0	0	0	0
7	10	9	12	9	4	12	6	10	10	7	0	0	0	0	0	0	0
7	8	8	4	4	6	2	2	4	2	4	0	0	0	0	0	0	0
2	2	2	0	0	0	2	2	4	4	6	6	8	8	8	8	8	8
0	0	0	0	0	0	0	0	0	0	0	0	0	0	0	0	0	0
2	0	0	0	0	0	0	0	0	0	0	0	0	0	0	0	0	0
4	4	2	0	0	0	0	0	0	0	0	0	0	0	0	0	0	0
4	4	4	2	0	0	0	0	0	0	0	0	0	0	0	0	0	0
8	8	8	9	9	9	10	10	J	J	J	Q	Q	Q	K	K	K	
7	7	8	8	9	9	9	10	10	J	J	J	Q	Q	Q	K		
6	7	7	8	8	9	9	9	10	10	10	J	J	J	Q	Q	K	
6	6	7	7	8	8	8	9	9	9	10	10	10	J	J	J	Q	
10	12	12	12	12	10	8	8	8	8	8	8	8	8	8	8	8	8

FOUR OF A KIND

Value Held	Cards Held	If Starter is: value added is:													Average Val. added is:		Average Total Count	
		A	2	3	4	5	6	7	8	9	10	J	Q	K	Units	48ths	Units	48ths
12	A A A A	—	0	0	0	0	0	0	0	0	0	0	0	0	0	0	12	0
12	2 2 2 2	0	—	0	0	0	0	2	0	8	0	0	0	0	0	40	12	40
12	3 3 3 3	0	0	—	0	0	8	0	0	12	0	0	0	0	1	32	13	32
12	4 4 4 4	0	0	8	—	0	0	12	0	0	0	0	0	0	1	32	13	32
20	5 5 5 5	0	0	0	0	—	0	0	0	0	8	8	8	8	2	32	22	32
12	6 6 6 6	0	0	12	0	0	—	0	0	8	0	0	0	0	1	32	13	32
12	7 7 7 7	12	0	0	0	0	0	—	8	0	0	0	0	0	1	32	13	32
12	8 8 8 8	0	0	0	0	0	0	8	—	0	0	0	0	0	0	32	12	32
12	9 9 9 9	0	0	0	0	0	8	0	0	—	0	0	0	0	0	32	12	32
12	10 10 10 10	0	0	0	0	8	0	0	0	0	—	0	0	0	0	32	12	32
12	J J J J	0	0	0	0	8	0	0	0	0	0	—	0	0	0	32	12	32
12	Q Q Q Q	0	0	0	0	8	0	0	0	0	0	0	—	0	0	32	12	32
12	K K K K	0	0	0	0	8	0	0	0	0	0	0	0	—	0	32	12	32

PAIRS ROYAL

Value Held	Cards Held	A	2	3	4	5	6	7	8	9	10	J	Q	K	Average Val. added is: Units	48ths	Average Total Count Units	48ths
														value added is:				
6	A A A 2	6	2	9	0	0	0	0	0	0	2	2	2	2	1	32	7	32
6	3	6	9	2	0	0	0	0	0	2	6	6	6	6	3	8	9	8
6	4	6	0	0	2	0	0	0	2	6	6	6	6	6	2	44	8	44
6	5	6	0	0	0	2	0	2	6	6	2	2	2	2	2	4	8	4
6	6	6	0	0	0	0	4	6	6	2	0	0	0	0	1	26	7	26
6	7	6	0	0	0	2	6	8	2	0	0	0	0	0	1	22	7	22
6	8	6	0	0	2	6	6	2	2	0	0	0	0	0	1	28	7	28
6	9	6	0	2	6	6	2	0	0	2	0	0	0	0	1	28	7	28
6	10,Q,K	6	2	6	6	2	0	0	0	0	2	0	0	0	1	28	7	28
6	J	6	2	6	6	2	0	0	0	0	0	2	0	0	1	39	7	39
6	2 2 2 A	2	6	9	0	0	0	0	2	2	6	6	6	6	3	16	9	16
6	3	9	6	2	9	0	2	0	6	2	6	6	6	6	4	28	10	28
6	4	0	6	9	2	2	0	6	0	8	0	0	0	0	2	16	8	16
6	5	0	6	0	2	2	6	0	6	2	2	2	2	2	2	12	8	12

PAIRS ROYAL (Continued)

Value Held	Cards Held	If Starter is: A	2	3	4	5	6	7	8	9	10	J	Q	K	Average Value added is: Units	48ths	Average Total Count Units	48ths
		value added is:																
6	6	0	6	2	0	6	2	6	0	4	0	0	0	0	1	36	7	36
6	7	0	8	0	6	0	6	2	2	2	0	0	0	0	1	30	7	30
6	8	2	6	6	0	6	0	2	2	2	0	0	0	0	1	36	7	36
8	9	0	12	0	6	0	2	0	0	4	0	0	0	0	1	8	9	8
6	10,Q,K	6	6	6	0	2	0	0	0	2	2	0	0	0	1	28	7	28
6	J	6	6	6	0	2	0	0	0	2	2	2	0	0	1	39	7	39
6 3 3 3	A	2	9	0	2	0	2	0	6	6	0	0	0	0	2	16	8	16
6	2	9	2	6	11	0	2	6	0	6	6	6	6	6	5	4	11	4
6	4	0	11	6	2	15	2	0	6	6	0	0	0	0	3	28	9	28
6	5	2	0	6	15	2	2	6	0	6	2	2	2	2	3	24	9	24
8	6	0	0	12	0	10	0	0	8	0	0	0	0	0	1	26	9	26
6	7	0	6	6	0	6	2	2	2	6	0	0	0	0	2	4	8	4
6	8	6	0	6	6	0	2	0	2	6	0	0	0	0	2	4	8	4
12	9	0	0	12	0	4	0	0	8	0	8	0	0	0	1	4	13	4

Count	Mark	Card														A	B	C	D
6		10,Q,K	0	0	0	2	6	0	2	2	2	6	6	6	0	28	7	28	1
6		J	0	0	2	0	6	0	2	2	2	6	6	6	0	39	7	39	1
6	4	A	6	6	6	6	0	0	6	6	0	6	2	2	2	28	9	28	3
6	4	2	0	0	0	0	0	0	6	0	6	6	11	2	2	40	8	40	2
8	4	3	0	0	0	0	0	6	6	0	9	12	4	9	0	0	11	0	3
6		5	2	2	2	2	0	0	6	15	2	6	11	6	0	4	10	4	4
6		6	0	0	0	0	2	0	8	2	15	6	2	6	6	40	8	40	2
12		7	0	0	0	0	0	2	8	0	0	12	2	0	0	4	13	4	1
6		8	0	0	0	0	0	2	6	0	0	6	8	0	0	28	7	28	1
6		9	0	0	0	0	2	0	6	2	2	6	2	0	0	28	7	28	1
8		10,Q,K	0	0	0	2	0	0	6	0	2	6	2	6	6	28	7	28	1
8		J	0	0	2	0	0	0	6	0	2	6	2	0	6	39	7	39	1
8	5	A	6	6	6	6	6	0	0	0	12	6	0	0	2	18	11	18	3
8	5	2	6	6	6	6	0	6	0	0	12	0	6	2	0	18	11	18	3
8	5	3	6	6	6	6	0	0	6	0	12	9	2	6	0	6	12	6	4
8	5	4	6	6	6	6	0	0	0	15	2	2	9	0	6	42	12	42	4
8		6	6	6	6	6	2	0	9	2	12	15	0	0	0	26	12	26	4
8		7	6	6	6	6	0	2	2	9	12	0	6	0	0	38	11	38	3
8		8	6	6	6	6	0	2	2	0	12	0	0	6	0	2	11	2	3

PAIRS ROYAL (Continued)

Value Held	Cards Held	If Starter is: value added is: A	2	3	4	5	6	7	8	9	10	J	Q	K	Average Value added is: Units	48ths	Average Total Count Units	48ths
8	9	6	0	0	0	0	2	0	0	2	6	6	6	6	3	2	11	2
14	10,Q,K	6	0	0	0	14	0	0	0	0	8	6	6	6	2	14	16	14
14	J	6	0	0	0	14	0	0	0	0	6	8	6	6	2	25	16	25
6	6 6 6 A	2	6	6	0	0	6	0	6	6	6	0	0	0	2	12	8	12
6	2	6	2	6	0	0	6	6	0	6	0	0	0	0	2	12	8	12
12	3	0	0	8	0	12	0	0	0	6	0	0	0	0	1	12	13	12
6	4	0	0	6	2	15	6	0	0	6	0	0	0	0	2	24	8	24
6	5	0	0	6	15	2	0	0	0	0	0	0	0	2	3	44	9	44
6	6	0	6	6	9	6	9	6	0	6	0	0	2	0	3	20	9	20
6	7	6	0	6	0	0	6	2	11	6	2	0	0	0	3	32	9	32
6	8	6	0	6	0	0	8	11	2	0	0	0	0	0	2	32	8	32
12	9	0	0	6	0	0	0	0	0	8	0	0	0	0	1	8	13	8
6	10,Q,K	0	6	6	0	2	6	0	0	6	0	2	0	0	1	20	7	20
6	J	0	0	6	0	2	6	0	0	6	2	0	0	0	1	31	7	31
12	7 7 7 A	8	0	0	0	0	0	12	6	6	0	0	0	0	1	12	13	12
6	2	6	2	0	0	0	6	6	6	6	0	0	0	0	1	36	7	36

Card																			
3		6	6	0	2	0	6	0	6	6	0	0	0	0	0	1	36	7	36
4		6	6	0	0	8	0	0	6	6	0	0	0	0	0	1	30	7	30
5		6	6	0	6	0	2	9	6	6	0	0	0	0	0	3	8	9	8
6		6	6	6	0	0	9	2	6	15	2	2	2	2	2	3	20	9	20
8		12	6	0	0	0	0	9	8	8	2	0	0	0	0	2	32	14	32
9		6	6	0	0	0	0	2	6	15	0	0	0	0	0	2	8	8	8
10,Q,K		6	6	0	0	0	2	0	6	6	2	2	0	0	0	1	20	7	20
J	8 8 8 / 8	6	6	0	0	0	2	0	6	6	0	0	2	0	0	1	31	7	31
A–4		6	2	2	0	0	0	6	6	6	0	0	0	0	0	1	12	7	12
5		6	0	0	0	0	2	0	6	6	0	2	2	2	2	1	44	7	44
6		6	6	6	0	0	0	2	15	6	2	0	2	2	2	2	8	8	8
7		12	0	0	0	0	0	9	8	8	9	0	0	0	0	2	8	14	8
9		6	0	0	0	0	0	2	15	6	2	0	0	0	0	2	20	8	20
10		6	0	0	0	0	2	0	6	6	9	9	0	0	0	1	32	7	32
J		6	0	0	0	0	2	0	6	6	0	2	2	0	0	1	7	7	7
Q,K		6	0	0	0	0	2	0	6	6	0	0	0	2	0	0	44	6	44
A	9 9 9 / 9	6	2	0	0	6	6	6	0	0	6	0	0	0	0	1	12	7	12
2		6	0	2	0	6	0	6	0	0	6	0	0	0	0	1	12	7	12
3		6	0	0	8	0	0	6	0	0	6	0	0	0	0	1	6	7	6

PAIRS ROYAL (Continued)

Value Held	Cards Held	If Starter is: value added is:													Average Val. added is:		Average Total Count	
		A	2	3	4	5	6	7	8	9	10	J	Q	K	Units	48ths	Units	48ths
6	4	0	6	0	2	0	6	0	0	6	6	0	0	0	1	12	7	12
6	5	6	0	0	0	2	6	0	0	6	2	2	2	2	1	44	7	44
12	6	0	0	0	0	0	8	0	0	8	0	0	0	0	0	32	12	32
6	7	0	0	0	0	6	0	2	11	6	0	0	0	0	1	32	7	32
6	8	0	0	0	0	6	11	11	2	6	0	0	0	0	2	20	8	20
6	10	0	0	0	0	2	6	0	9	2	9	0	0	0	2	20	8	20
6	J	0	0	0	0	2	6	0	0	6	2	2	0	0	1	43	7	43
6	Q,K	0	0	0	2	6	6	0	0	6	0	0	2	2	0	44	6	44
6	10 10 10 A	2	2	6	6	0	0	0	0	0	0	0	0	0	1	12	7	12
6	2	0	0	6	0	6	0	0	0	0	6	0	0	0	1	12	7	12
6	3	6	6	2	0	6	0	0	0	0	6	0	0	0	1	12	7	12
6	4	6	0	6	2	6	0	0	0	0	6	0	0	0	1	12	7	12
12	5	0	8	0	0	0	0	0	0	8	8	2	2	2	1	8	13	8
6	6	0	0	0	0	6	2	2	0	6	2	0	0	0	0	44	6	44
6	7	0	0	0	0	0	0	0	2	0	6	0	0	0	0	44	6	44

Freq	Card														n_1	n_2	n_3	n_4
6	8	0	0	0	0	6	0	2	2	9	6	6	0	0	1	32	7	32
6	9	0	0	0	0	6	6	0	9	2	6	9	0	0	2	20	8	20
6	J	0	0	0	0	8	2	0	0	9	6	2	9	0	2	31	8	31
6	Q	0	0	0	0	8	0	0	0	0	6	9	2	0	1	32	7	32
6	K	0	0	0	0	8	0	0	0	0	6	0	0	2	0	44	6	44
6	A	2	0	0	6	6	0	0	0	0	0	6	0	0	1	47	7	47
6	2	0	2	6	0	6	0	0	0	0	0	6	0	0	1	47	7	47
6	3	0	6	2	0	6	0	0	0	0	0	6	0	0	1	47	7	47
6	4	6	0	0	2	6	0	0	0	0	0	6	0	0	1	47	7	47
12	5	0	0	0	0	8	0	0	0	2	2	8	2	2	1	43	13	43
6	6	0	0	0	0	6	2	0	0	0	0	6	0	0	1	31	7	31
6	7	0	0	0	0	6	0	2	2	0	0	6	0	0	1	31	7	31
6	8	0	0	0	0	6	0	2	2	2	0	6	0	0	1	31	7	31
6	9	0	0	0	0	6	2	0	0	9	9	6	0	0	2	19	8	19
6	10	0	0	0	0	8	0	0	0	9	2	6	9	0	3	7	9	7
6	Q	0	0	0	0	8	0	0	0	0	9	6	2	9	3	7	9	7
6	K	0	0	0	0	8	0	0	0	0	0	6	9	2	2	19	8	19
6	Q Q Q A—4	2	0	0	6	6	0	0	0	0	0	0	6	0	1	12	7	12
12	5	0	0	0	0	8	0	0	0	0	2	2	8	2	1	8	13	8

J J J

PAIRS ROYAL (Continued)

Value Held	Cards Held	If Starter is: A	2	3	4	5	6	7	8	9	10	J	Q	K	Average Val. added is: Units	48ths	Average Total Count Units	48ths
		value added is:																
6	6–9	0	0	0	0	6	2	0	0	2	0	0	6	0	0	44	6	44
6	10	0	0	0	0	8	0	0	0	0	9	9	6	0	1	32	7	32
6	J	0	0	0	0	8	0	0	0	0	9	2	6	9	2	31	8	31
6	K	0	0	0	0	8	0	0	0	0	0	9	6	2	1	32	7	32
K K K																		
6	A–4	Similar to above.													1	12	7	12
12	5	"													1	8	13	8
6	6–10	"													0	44	6	44
6	J	0	0	0	0	8	0	0	0	0	0	2	9	6	1	43	7	43
6	Q	0	0	0	0	8	0	0	0	0	9	2	6	6	1	32	7	32
TWO PAIRS																		
4	A A 2 2	4	4	12	0	0	0	0	0	0	2	4	4	4	2	40	6	40
4	A A 3 3	4	12	4	0	0	0	2	4	2	4	4	4	4	3	16	7	16
4	A A 4 4	4	0	0	4	2	4	0	4	4	8	8	8	8	4	0	8	0
4	A A 5 5	4	0	2	4	6	0	4	8	4	4	4	4	4	3	12	7	12

12	20	32	32	32	7	32	32	0	0	12	8	40	32	24	32	7	32	32
6	9	5	5	5	6	5	5	10	7	7	6	5	5	5	5	6	5	5
12	20	32	32	32	7	32	32	0	0	12	8	40	32	24	32	7	32	32
2	1	1	1	1	2	1	1	6	3	3	2	1	1	1	1	2	1	1
0	0	0	0	0	0	0	4	8	0	4	0	0	0	0	0	0	0	4
0	0	0	0	0	0	4	0	8	0	4	0	0	0	0	0	0	4	0
0	0	0	0	0	4	0	0	8	0	4	0	0	0	0	0	4	0	0
0	0	0	0	4	0	0	0	8	0	4	0	0	0	0	4	0	0	0
4	0	0	4	0	0	0	0	2	8	0	4	0	0	4	0	0	0	0
8	4	4	0	0	0	0	0	4	0	8	0	4	4	0	0	0	0	0
4	12	4	0	0	0	0	0	4	6	0	8	4	4	0	0	0	0	0
4	4	8	4	0	0	0	0	0	0	4	4	8	0	4	0	0	0	0
0	0	4	8	4	4	4	4	2	4	6	4	0	8	0	4	4	4	4
2	0	0	4	8	8	8	8	12	4	0	0	4	0	8	0	0	0	0
2	0	0	0	4	4	4	4	4	14	4	0	2	0	4	0	8	8	8
6	0	0	0	0	0	0	0	4	4	4	4	2	4	0	8	4	4	4
6	6	4	4	4	4	4	4	12	0	2	4	2	0	0	4	4	4	4
6	7	8	9	10	J	Q	K	3	4	5	6	7	8	9	10	J	Q	K
6	7	8	9	10	J	Q	K	3	4	5	6	7	8	9	10	J	Q	K
A	A	A	A	A	A	A	A	2	2	2	2	2	2	2	2	2	2	2
A	A	A	A	A	A	A	A	2	2	2	2	2	2	2	2	2	2	2
4	8	4	4	4	4	4	4	4	4	4	4	4	4	4	4	4	4	4

PAIRS

Value Held	Cards Held				If Starter is: A	2	3	4	5	6	7	8	9	10	J	Q	K	Average Val. added is: Units	48ths	Average Total Count Units	48ths
					value added is:																
4	2	2	3	3	12	4	4	12	2	0	4	4	2	8	8	8	8	6	0	10	0
4	2	2	4	4	0	4	14	4	4	0	6	0	8	0	0	0	4	3	0	7	0
4	2	2	5	5	2	4	4	0	6	4	0	8	0	4	4	4	4	3	12	7	12
4	2	2	6	6	4	4	2	0	4	4	8	0	4	0	0	0	0	2	8	6	8
4	2	2	7	7	2	4	0	4	0	8	4	4	0	0	0	0	0	1	40	5	40
4	2	2	8	8	0	4	4	0	8	0	4	4	0	0	0	0	0	1	32	5	32
4	2	2	9	9	0	8	0	8	0	4	0	0	4	0	0	0	0	1	24	5	24
4	2	2	10	10	4	4	8	0	4	0	0	0	0	4	4	0	0	1	32	5	32
4	2	2	J	J	2	2	8	0	4	0	0	0	0	4	0	4	0	2	7	6	7
4	2	2	Q	Q	4	4	8	0	4	0	0	0	0	0	0	4	4	1	32	5	32
4	2	2	K	K	2	4	8	0	4	0	0	0	0	0	0	0	4	1	32	5	32
4	3	3	4	4	2	12	4	8	16	0	2	8	2	0	0	0	0	4	0	8	0
4	3	3	5	5	0	4	4	16	6	0	8	0	2	4	4	4	4	4	12	8	12
8	3	3	6	6	0	0	10	0	0	12	0	0	6	0	0	0	0	1	20	9	20
4	3	3	7	7	2	4	4	0	8	0	4	4	2	0	0	0	0	2	0	6	0

40	4	24	47	24	24	12	0	12	24	24	24	47	24	24	44	44	36	36
5	9	5	5	5	5	9	7	9	5	5	5	5	5	5	8	7	6	6
40	4	24	47	24	24	12	0	12	24	24	24	47	24	24	44	44	36	36
1	1	1	1	1	1	5	3	1	1	1	1	1	1	1	4	3	2	2
0	0	0	0	0	4	4	0	0	0	0	0	0	0	4	4	4	4	4
0	0	0	0	4	0	4	0	0	0	0	0	0	4	0	4	4	4	4
0	0	0	4	0	0	4	0	0	0	0	0	4	0	0	4	4	4	4
0	0	4	0	0	0	4	0	0	0	0	4	0	0	0	4	4	4	4
2	6	2	2	2	2	0	4	0	0	4	0	0	0	0	4	0	0	4
4	0	0	0	0	0	0	0	4	4	0	0	0	0	0	0	4	4	0
0	0	0	0	0	0	2	2	6	6	2	2	2	2	2	12	4	4	0
0	4	0	0	0	0	20	4	0	0	4	0	0	0	0	4	12	4	0
0	0	4	4	4	4	6	20	0	0	0	4	4	4	4	6	6	6	6
8	0	0	0	0	0	4	4	12	4	4	4	4	4	4	20	0	0	0
4	12	4	4	4	4	12	2	0	8	0	0	0	0	0	2	8	0	0
0	0	8	8	8	8	4	0	0	0	8	0	0	0	0	0	2	8	0
4	0	0	0	0	0	4	4	2	0	0	8	8	8	8	0	2	0	8
8	9	10	J	Q	K	5	6	7	8	9	10	J	Q	K	6	7	8	9
8	9	10	J	Q	K	5	6	7	8	9	10	J	Q	K	6	7	8	9
3	3	3	3	3	3	4	4	4	4	4	4	4	4	4	5	5	5	5
3	3	3	3	3	3	4	4	4	4	4	4	4	4	4	5	5	5	5
4	8	4	4	4	4	4	4	8	4	4	4	4	4	4	4	4	4	4

PAIRS

Value Held	Cards Held	A	2	3	4	5	6	7	8	9	10	J	Q	K	Average Val. added is: Units	48ths	Average Total Count Units	48ths
		value added is:																
12	5 5 10 10	0	0	0	0	10	0	0	0	0	8	4	4	4	1	36	13	36
12	5 5 J J	0	0	0	0	10	0	0	0	0	4	8	4	4	2	11	14	11
12	5 5 Q Q	0	0	0	0	10	0	0	0	0	4	4	8	4	1	36	13	36
12	5 5 K K	0	0	0	0	10	0	0	0	0	4	4	4	8	1	36	13	36
4	6 6 7 7	2	8	2	0	12	4	4	16	4	0	0	0	0	4	0	8	0
4	6 6 8 8	8	0	2	0	0	4	16	4	4	0	0	0	0	2	40	6	40
12	6 6 9 9	0	0	2	0	0	8	0	0	8	0	0	0	0	0	40	12	40
4	6 6 10 10	0	0	2	0	4	4	0	0	4	4	0	0	0	1	8	5	8
4	6 6 J J	0	0	2	0	4	4	0	0	4	0	4	0	0	1	31	5	31
4	6 6 Q Q	0	0	2	0	4	4	0	0	4	0	0	4	0	1	8	5	8
4	6 6 K K	0	0	2	0	4	4	0	0	4	0	0	0	4	1	8	5	8
12	7 7 8 8	2	0	0	0	0	12	8	8	12	0	0	0	0	2	40	14	40
4	7 7 9 9	2	0	0	0	0	4	4	16	4	0	0	0	0	2	8	6	8
4	7 7 10 10	2	0	0	0	4	0	4	4	0	4	0	0	0	1	8	5	8

4	7	7	J	2	0	0	4	0	4	4	0	0	4	0	0	1	31	5	31
4	7	7	Q	2	0	0	4	0	4	4	0	0	0	4	0	1	8	5	8
4	7	7	K	2	0	0	4	0	4	4	0	0	0	0	4	1	8	5	8
4	8	8	9	0	0	0	0	4	16	4	4	12	0	0	0	3	0	7	0
4	8	8	10	0	0	0	4	0	4	4	12	4	0	0	0	2	0	6	0
4	8	8	J	0	0	0	4	0	4	4	0	0	4	0	0	1	23	5	23
4	8	8	Q	0	0	0	4	0	4	4	0	0	0	4	0	1	0	5	0
4	8	8	K	0	0	0	4	0	4	4	0	0	0	0	4	1	0	5	0
4	9	9	10	0	0	0	4	4	0	12	4	4	12	0	0	3	23	7	23
4	9	9	J	0	0	0	4	4	0	0	4	12	4	0	0	2	0	6	0
4	9	9	Q	0	0	0	4	4	0	0	4	0	0	4	0	1	0	5	0
4	9	9	K	0	0	0	4	4	0	0	0	0	0	0	4	1	23	5	23
4	10	10	J	0	0	0	8	0	0	0	12	4	4	0	0	3	0	7	0
4	10	10	Q	0	0	0	8	0	0	0	0	4	4	12	0	2	0	6	0
4	10	10	K	0	0	0	8	0	0	0	0	12	4	4	4	1	23	5	23
4	J	J	Q	0	0	0	8	0	0	0	0	0	12	4	12	3	23	7	23
4	J	J	K	0	0	0	8	0	0	0	0	0	0	12	4	2	23	6	23
4	Q	Q	K	0	0	0	8	0	0	0	0	0	12	4	4	2	0	6	0